ALEXANDER CAMPBELL

Leader of the Great Reformation
of the Nineteenth Century

by
THOMAS W. GRAFTON

COBB PUBLISHING
2017

Cobb Publishing
704 E. Main Street
Charleston, AR 72933
(479) 747-8372

CobbPublishing@gmail.com
www.CobbPublishing.com

This book has been completely reformatted, edited, and corrected to give you the best possible reading experience.

A free digital copy of this book is available from the Jimmie Beller Memorial eLibrary, located at www.TheCobbSix.com.

ISBN-13: 978-1947622050
ISBN-10: 1947622056

Table of Contents

PREFACE

The richest heritage of any people is in the lives and memories of the good and great who have preceded them. This is especially true of those who have helped to the possession of new lands, or the discovery of new truths, or the establishment of new principles.

Such a heritage the young people of our Endeavor Societies have in the leaders of the religious movement which, in the early part of this century, led to the establishment of the Christian Church. Though the history of that movement does not yet span a century, no religious body has a richer calendar of saints than we. Many of them may have been lacking in the conventional graces of society, and in high scholastic attainments; but in the genuineness of their sympathies and in their familiarity with God's two great books—nature and the Bible—all were, in the highest and truest sense, gentlemen and scholars.

First among these worthies must ever be placed that grand man, to whose faith, originality, and genius our religious movement owes its origin, Alexander Campbell, the Sage of Bethany. To bring the story of his life within a compass that would enable busy people to become acquainted with him, has been the end sought in this volume. With a literature so rich in material, this has been no small task. The sixty volumes which grew up under the genius of Mr. Campbell, including the Christian Baptist and Millennial Harbinger, are rich in biographical suggestion. In addition to these the author is indebted to Dr. Richardson's valuable "Memoirs." All he claims is to have gathered, from these sources, the most important events in this great life, and to have compressed them within a space that may encourage every lover of truth to sit, for a season, at the feet of one of its most earnest defenders.

INTRODUCTION

The time has not yet come when Mr. Campbell can be fairly measured and assigned his true place in Christian history. There are those among his admirers who regard him as the greatest religious teacher of the century; others, animated by the antagonisms of earlier days, or not especially acquainted with his work or the people he rallied to the platform of Christian unity, would deny him any conspicuous place among the makers of modern Christian thought. Somewhere between these positions the truth lies, but we are yet too near the man himself to secure a true perspective. It is only fair to say, however, that those who knew most of Mr. Campbell's life and work, and have the largest admiration for him, await with confidence the verdict of the future.

Meantime there is no question that he was a true prophet of his time. It is the privilege of some men to perceive the greatest needs of the Church of Christ in their day, to give happy and forceful expression to thoughts that are lying unexpressed in the minds of many around them, and by vigorous advocacy call the attention of scattered sections of the church to the truth they have discerned. This is the function of a true prophet of Christianity. It was the work of Mr. Campbell. He did not create the idea of Christian unity. Many minds had grappled with it since the Reformation caused the great breach in the Church. The reformers themselves felt the dangers of division and sought to heal the rents in their forces. Protestants and Romanists worked at the problem, as the correspondence of Leibnitz and Bossuet witnesses. The labors of Richard Baxter in England, who organized associations for the cultivation of unity among Christians, and wrote pamphlets to the same end, are representative of what many men in different places were seeking to realize. Milton's dream of a simpler faith and a more united church dawned upon other minds. It is a commonplace of our history that other movements in America for freedom and apostolic Christianity preceded Mr. Campbell's work. He did not create the idea, but he gave it the first full expression and adjusted it to other questions whose relation to it was intimate.

Mr. Campbell was convinced, both by his own observations and the experiences of his father in Britain and America, that the greatest hindrance to the progress and success of the church was the lack of unity. Power that should have been employed in combating sin and bringing in larger measure the Kingdom of God was wasted in sectarian strife. But the desired unity among the followers of Jesus was not to be secured by the mere proclamation of its desirability. It must be sought by a return to apostolic standards of thought, speech, and conduct. It was not an attempt to reproduce the faulty and partial life of the churches in Jerusalem, Corinth, Galatia, or Rome to which Mr. Campbell set himself and rallied his friends.

It was an appeal to Christ and to apostolic standards of teaching and conduct. On such a platform it was believed Christians could unite in the service of the common Lord. The principles accepted by all believers as essential to fellowship with the Savior were regarded sufficient as a bond of union. Convinced that peace could be restored to the divided church only by a restoration of the apostolic program, Mr. Campbell labored to secure a larger acquaintance with the New Testament on the part of all who would cooperate in healing the divisions of the Church. The New Testament was seen to be the rule of belief and conduct, and to it, as the law and testimony, the appeal was evermore made. This will explain the fact that Mr. Campbell gave more attention to the subject of Apostolic Christianity and its re-establishment than he did to Christian Union. In his plan the one was the necessary antecedent of the other.

While Mr. Campbell exhibited a high degree of mental independence, and departed to a startling degree from the established religious customs of his time, he was a true child of his period in his ways of thinking, and the formative influences about him in early life are distinctly discerned through his entire career. Chief among these are to be named the sterling characteristics inherited from generations of sturdy Scotch and Huguenot ancestors; the atmosphere of a Christian home in which the highest regard for Divine things was maintained; the supremacy of the philosophy of John Locke in the thinking of the time, with its rejection of Cartesianism, its appeal to fact, its theory of knowledge as the result of sensation, thus becoming the foundation of the Scotch School of philosophy and the precursor of Berkeley and Hume, Reid and Hartley, and whose influence is traceable in the Encyclopedists and Kant; the impress of the Covenant Theology, that modification of Calvinism, brought from Holland, and widely diffused through Scotland after the Secession, with its insistence upon a progress of revelation in the Bible marked by Covenants; the principles of the Independents, represented on different sides by Glas, Sandeman, Walker, Hill, and the Haldanes; lastly the divided condition of the churches in Scotland and Ireland, where Presbyterianism was broken into a score of fragments, not to speak of other communions; all these forces wrought in the making of Mr. Campbell.

Of some of them he was conscious, and expressed his indebtedness, as to Locke. Of others he seems to have been unaware, or at least not impressed with a sense of obligation. Especially is this true of his theological views. Yet no man ever made more free and independent use of the material at hand. It was this singular combination of elements, native and acquired, together with a deep earnestness in seeking to be led by the Spirit of God, that made him distinctively the prophet of his time.

The place of the Disciples of Christ among the religious forces of the time is one of growing importance. Much has been done to widen the influence of the propaganda in behalf of Christian unity. This sentiment is one of the watchwords of the hour, and without claiming the entire credit for this condition, the Disciples may fairly discern one of the causes in their labors. But the work is not done. The result has not yet been attained, and the plans for reaching it are almost as varied as the sections of the church. It ought to be in such a time as this that the maturing energies of the Disciples may be applied with fresh vigor to the problem.

The desirability of closer unity among God's people is no

longer an open question. How can it be attained? It is believed that the apostolic program furnishes a sufficient basis for fellowship, and that in the courteous but persistent advocacy of this method of unity the Disciples find a sufficient and imperative sanction for their message to the world. Only by such advocacy can they be true, not alone to the memory of Mr. Campbell and his associates, but to the platform of New Testament Christianity, which is of infinitely greater importance.

The present volume is a contribution to a larger knowledge of Mr. Campbell and his times. Few have leisure or opportunity to read Richardson's two volumes, and, moreover, much may now be added to the subject which was not then accessible. This book ought to result in a largely increased acquaintance with the beginnings of the movement, and help many among the Disciples of Christ to vindicate afresh the position which they occupy among the religious forces of the time.

Herbert L. Willett.
Disciples' Divinity House,
Chicago.

Chapter One:
EARLY DAYS

The author of a religious movement which, within the space of three-quarters of a century, can claim a million adherents is deserving of the consideration of all thoughtful people. When that movement rises, not on the tide of popular favor, but in the face of the most bitter opposition, the genius that could inspire it is doubly deserving of our attention. Such have been the trials and triumphs of the Christian Church, which, with its vast membership and multiplied agencies for the regeneration of the world, is today a monument to the faith and genius of Alexander Campbell, and which assures him an exalted place among the world's religious leaders.

The village of Ballymena, nestled among the hills of Northern Ireland, furnishes the starting point for the life-story I am to tell. Just beyond its borders was a humble cottage, surrounded by a few acres of land, in which, more than a hundred years ago, two worthy young people, Thomas and Jane Campbell, began life with a noble ancestry, and brought into that home a treasure of more value than wealth or title, a deep religious purpose and sterling qualities of character which shine with splendor wherever found.

Thomas Campbell had descended from that valiant Scotch stock, the Campbells of Argyle, which covered itself with glory in the days of Scotland's political and religious struggles. Some two or three generations prior to his birth, his branch of the family had emigrated to Northern Ireland, where, though not distinguished, it maintained its integrity, and gave to society many valuable members. Jane Corneigle, to whom Thomas Campbell was wedded in 1787, was of no less worthy descent. Her ancestors were Huguenots, who, in those terrible days of persecution that followed the revocation of the Edict of Nantes, had chosen exile from their beloved France rather than surrender their faith. After their settlement in Ireland her people were the devoted friends of liberal education, establishing and fostering schools, where the Bible, along with the common branches, was carefully taught. Both, thus endowed by birth, were of the stuff suited to the hardships through which they were destined afterward to pass.

At the time of the birth of their first-born, Alexander, in 1788, the future offered little encouragement to them. Thomas Campbell had already dedicated himself to the work of the ministry, but, in the interval of preparation for that work, he was compelled to devote his energies largely to school teaching, with meager compensation, combining with the duties of teacher, as opportunity afforded, the work of ministering to the spiritual needs of his neighbors. He was Presbyterian in faith, having at an early age identified himself with the Seceders, a branch of that church. His mind from youth was one of deep religious cast. There had early been developed a sincere and earnest love for the Scriptures. As the claims of a religious life began to present themselves, he passed through that intense mental agony which was then thought to be indispensable in seeking acceptance with God. When at last his doubts and fears were dissipated, it was as if his whole nature was flooded with the sunlight of God's love. From that moment he felt himself wholly called of God, and henceforth dedicated to his work, and bent all his energies to the training of mind and heart for a life of service in the ministry. As was to be expected, the home-life of a nature so deeply religious but reflected his loyalty and devotion to the Christ.

It will be seen that the early life of Alexander Campbell found its development in an intensely religious Atmosphere. In the family, Christ was something more than a name. He was an abiding Guest, and his Word was a treasure whose aroma filled the home with fragrance. A part of the home regime was the daily memorizing of the Scriptures by the younger members of the family. In this way young Campbell was brought up to regard with profound reverence the Word of God, the logical sequence of which was his great life-work of seeking to restore it to its rightful place.

The exalted ideal of Thomas Campbell is seen in his refusal to thrust the family in the way of temptation for the sake of gain. While battling with adversity, he was offered the position of tutor in the family of the Governor-General of Ireland, with a large salary and an elegant residence; but the offer was promptly declined, lest it should endanger the morals of his children by placing before them the fascinations of worldly pride and fashion.

When Alexander was about ten years of age, the family, after many vicissitudes, was established on a farm near the city of Armagh, in the midst of the field of labor to which Thomas Campbell had been called as pastor. The region is described as one of the most beautiful of Ireland. Its rich farms, its lofty hills, its secluded valleys, its sparkling lakes, presented a scene of varied and untiring beauty. Here the boyhood of Alexander was chiefly spent and the foundation of his great learning laid. It is to be presumed that the father and mother, devoted as they were to the highest interests of their children, were his first instructors. But with the increasing duties of his pastorate, the father found it necessary to make other provision for the instruction of his son. Determined that he should not lack opportunity for gaining an education, he was sent to such schools as the vicinity afforded, and later put in an academy, then conducted by his uncles, Archibald and Enos, in the town of Newry, some ten miles distant.

At this period the future reformer manifested none of those traits of intellectual superiority that afterward distinguished him. His rather over-fondness for sports seems to have interfered seriously with his educational progress. He loved the freedom of outdoor life better than his books. A rod and line had much more attraction for him than the daily tasks of the schoolroom. Study became a drudgery, and his persistent negligence filled his father with deep concern. The one anecdote related of his boyhood illustrates both his own indifference and his father's impatience. The French language had been added to his other studies, and on a warm day he sought the shade of a tree as the most suitable place to prepare his lesson in "The Adventures of Telemachus." Falling asleep and dropping his book in the grass, he was unconscious of the approach of a cow, until the animal had seized and actually devoured the book. Upon reporting the loss, his father not only severely punished him for his carelessness, but further reprimanded him by telling him that "the cow had got more French in her stomach than he had in his head," a fact which he was not then able to deny. As a last resort, his anxious father, "to break him into his books," determined to put him to work on the farm. He was consequently taken from school and sent to the field. The plan at first seemed destined to miscarry. The change pleased Alexander. He loved the farm. His heart, tender and fresh, beat a responsive note to nature, and he was for the time satisfied with the calling that brought him near to nature's heart. The years thus spent in healthful physical labor were, however, not misspent. They proved to be no small factor in the making of the man, and in his equipment for the place he was ultimately to occupy as a leader of men; for under the invigorating influence of outdoor life he gained in health and vigor, laying the foundation of that iron constitution that served him so well in the unremitting labors of later years.

There is a critical period in every young life, which, safely passed, gives promise of a career of usefulness, but which, beset as it is with foes, often leads to disaster. At this dividing of the ways, Alexander Campbell, a youth of some sixteen summers, had now arrived. His future hung upon the course chosen. It was with anxious, prayerful solicitude that his father watched the result, and with justifiable pride that he discovered an awakening thirst for knowledge in the growing boy. His intellectual nature, which he possessed in rich endowment, at last began to assert its claims. The books which had been thrown aside were taken up with renewed interest. A desire for literary distinction possessed him, and he confidentially declared his purpose to become "one of the best scholars of the kingdom."

The pathway along which he now bent his steps was not easy of pursuit. The educational advantages of the community in which he lived were limited, the family resources meager, and a course at the university apparently beyond his reach. But in this emergency the resources of the father were not wanting. He supplied the lack of larger opportunities by personally superintending his son's intellectual development. What an encouraging example these two present, father and son in loving companionship, courageously surmounting all barriers, that they may quaff together the sweet waters of the perennial spring of truth! But for the wisdom of the father in this struggle, the world had in all probability been robbed of the splendid achievements of the son.

At this fireside university the traits of mind that afterward were so conspicuous in the genius of Alexander Campbell began to display themselves. They were intense mental activity, an unquenchable thirst for knowledge, and a remarkably quick and retentive memory. His power to grasp and retain the results of his reading has been surpassed by but few men. It is related of him at this early period that, as a test, he committed to memory sixty lines of blank verse in fifty-two minutes, so that he could repeat them without missing a word. But this remarkable power, which he retained through life, was not the mere accident of genius. It was the result of the most painstaking effort. To develop this faculty he accustomed himself to daily memorizing extracts from the best authors, and thus, early in youth, beside the mental discipline gained, his mind became a storehouse of the best thought and the most chaste language of English literature. As a further aid to memory and thoughtful reading, it was his custom to copy in his notebook extracts from his reading, passages which particularly pleased him. In this way he provided that intellectual furnishing which gave beauty and power to his uttered thought.

The process by which he was now being trained in scholarly pursuits was necessarily slow. Such was the occupation of the father that interruptions often occurred. The duty of attending to the spiritual needs of the church to which he faithfully ministered, besides looking after and providing for a large family, left little time for this labor of love. And now that the family wants might be supplied, it became necessary for the father to supplement his meager salary as pastor by a return to the schoolroom. A suitable location for an academy having been found in the village of Rich Hill, two miles distant from the parish to which he had for several years ministered, he removed his family thither, and soon witnessed the growth of a flourishing school. All this made heavy demands upon his time; but, notwithstanding, he managed to perfect his son in the preliminary English branches, and to give him such instruction in Latin and Greek as would enable him, should opportunity ever present itself, to enter the classes of the university.

That this work might go on, it became necessary for Alexander to come to his father's relief by rendering such assistance as he could in the academy. So thorough was his mastery of the common branches, that at the age of seventeen he proved himself a most competent teacher and valuable assistant. But while occupied with the daily cares of the schoolroom, he did not allow himself, for a moment, to swerve from his purpose of gaining an education. He pursued with unflagging energy his own special course of studies, still under his father's guidance. As the seed-time of life, he felt the importance of every moment of sowing, and therefore availed himself of every accessible source of knowledge, as well as every fragment of time. While others slept, he communed with the spirit of learning. During these busy days he was accustomed to pursue his studies far into the night, and usually arose at four in the morning to resume them. The work of self-education, the only educational privilege he seemed likely ever to enjoy, thus became a passion with him.

But to imagine that the old buoyancy of his nature had been vanquished in this passion is to mistake the temper of the youth. Along with his love of intellectual pursuits, but always hereafter in subjection to it, he carried his intense fondness for outdoor sports. His athletic frame made him a favorite among his companions in physical contests of the times, which to the young people of today would seem rather strange forms of amusement. He was famed for the size of the snow-balls he could make and the force with which he hurled them in their playful battles. Among the farmers of the neighborhood he easily carried off the championship in sowing grain, an exercise of which he was fond and an art in which he was expert. But along with these antiquated amusements, he also delighted in the use of rod and gun, proving himself an Isaak Walton and Nimrod, both in one. It was by these healthful diversions that he was able to pursue his arduous labors in the schoolroom and the study, with unimpaired physical vigor.

With the unfolding of mind came the consideration of those serious problems which always present themselves for solution where the Word of God is known. From a youth, Alexander had known and revered the Scriptures. As we have already seen, an important part of the family life was its daily study. Its message had been brought home to him through the worthy example of pious parents. His father, who had become his inseparable companion, was "a pattern of good works," admired and beloved by all who knew him. His mother exerted a no less molding influence upon his religious character. Long after her death, in his declining years, he paid this tribute to her memory:

> *She made a nearer approximation to the acknowledged beau ideal of a Christian mother than any one of her sex with whom I have had the pleasure of forming a special acquaintance. I can but gratefully add, that to my mother, as well as to my father, I am indebted for having memorized in early life almost all the writings of King Solomon, his Proverbs, his Ecclesiastes, and many of the Psalms of his father David They have not only been written on the tablet of my memory, but incorporated with my modes of thinking and speaking.* [1]

In time he began to seriously meditate upon his own religious obligations. As his convictions deepened he became greatly concerned about his own salvation. Of his religious conflicts and triumphs at this period, he, many years afterward, gave the following account:

> *From the time that I could read the Scriptures, I became convinced that Jesus was the Son of God. I was also fully persuaded that I was a sinner and must obtain pardon through the merits of Christ or be lost forever. This caused me great distress of soul, and I*

---

[1] *Life of Thomas Campbell.*

had much exercise of mind under the awakenings of a guilty conscience. Finally, after many strugglings, I was enabled to put my trust in the Saviour and to feel my reliance on him as the only Saviour of sinners. From the moment I was able to feel this reliance on the Lord Jesus Christ, I obtained and enjoyed peace of mind. It never entered into my head to investigate the subject of baptism or the doctrines of the creed.[1]

With Alexander Campbell, this beginning of Christ's service was upon a religious basis that broadened and deepened with each increasing year, until it became the absorbing passion of his life, the flame that shot up illuminating his whole nature, the theme that never ceased to inspire his tongue and pen, and that to the end of his life consumed all his thought and energy. Having accepted Christ, he accepted him for service, and immediately united with the Presbyterian Church, to which his father ministered, that he might aid in its triumphs and contribute to his Master's praise.

---

[1] *Memoirs of Alexander Campbell*, Vol. 1, page 49.

Chapter Two:
UNIVERSITY LIFE

We come now to a series of circumstances that changed the whole current of Alexander Campbell's life, and made possible his dream of classic attainments. Misfortune after misfortune overtook his father's family, which, in the end, proved to be the leadings of Providence towards a complete preparation for the great work that was to consume his energies.

In the midst of the increasing duties of church and school at Rich Hill, the father's health gave way, threatening a termination of his career of usefulness. As a last resort, his physicians recommended a sea voyage, in consequence of which his mind turned towards the new world. But from such a step he naturally shrank. He was a man of warm nature and strong attachments, and the thought of severing old ties, and especially of separation for a time from his family, to whose welfare he was devoted, was painful to him, indeed. At this point, Alexander helped his father to a decision by declaring his own intention of emigrating to America as soon as he had attained his majority, and by further assuring him of his readiness to continue the school and look after the welfare of the family during his absence.

So, after much prayerful consideration and many misgivings, it was finally decided that Thomas Campbell should immediately embark upon the voyage across the Atlantic, and that as soon as a suitable location had been found in the new world, the other members of the family should follow. On this errand he started out, leaving his native land in the early spring of 1807. After a voyage, at that time reckoned as a remarkably quick one, of thirty-five days, he landed in Philadelphia, and immediately proceeded to Western Pennsylvania, whither several of his old neighbors had preceded him. Here he met with a hearty welcome, and found the conditions for a time favorable for the reception of truths he long had cherished as indispensable to the ultimate triumph of Christianity.

In the meantime, the cares and support of the large family

fell upon the shoulders of Alexander, who, though but an in-experienced youth of nineteen, assumed the new responsibili-ties with the wisdom and discretion of one of mature years. Among other duties which his father's departure placed upon him was the management of the Academy which he assumed until the close of the term. As months wore on and no ar-rangement had as yet been made for the removal of the family, Alexander, anxious to improve his time, accepted the position of assistant in the school conducted by his uncle Archibald, at Newry, some miles distant from his home village. While thus engaged, word came from his father, bringing assurance that a new home had been provided, and urging the family to make immediate preparation for the voyage. This was in March, 1808. But before the final preparation was completed, misfor-tune again overtook the Campbells. The community was visited by a scourge of small-pox, which invaded the Campbell home and delayed their departure until autumn. When all were con-valescent, another attempt was made to join the father, which at first promised to be successful. The family were permitted to embark on one of the slow sailing vessels of that time, for a long voyage, with a promised reunion, in the end, in a happy home in the new world.

But here another calamity befell them. They were scarcely out of the harbor of Lough Foyle, before a terrible gale swept the vessel in which they had sailed on to the rocky coast of Western Scotland. After three days of alarm and uncertainty, they were stranded upon a hidden rock, and left to the mercy of wind and wave. For hours the fortune of the ship was imperiled, no one knowing at what moment the vessel might go down. Signals of distress were given in vain, and all were in momen-tary expectation of death.

It was in the intense anguish of this awful hour that the fu-ture of Alexander Campbell was forged. Having done what he could for the safety and comfort of the family, he sat on the stump of a broken mast and abandoned himself to reflection. In the near prospect of death he awoke to an appreciation of the meaning and mission of earthly existence, and to the folly of earthly aim and ambition. Life came to him with new meaning, and its true object appeared as he had never before conceived it. Only one motive seemed worthy of human effort, and that was the salvation and everlasting happiness of mankind. It was then that he formed the resolution that, if saved from the threatening peril, he would give himself wholly to God and his service, and spend his entire life as a minister of the Word. While engaged in these solemn reflections, relief was unexpectedly brought to the distressed vessel. The inhabitants of a village on the neighboring shore were at last made aware of its peril, and by their heroic efforts rescued the entire company of the ill-fated ship, and gave them hospitable reception until provision could be made for the continuance of the voyage.

This disaster, besides leading to the decision that secured to the world the invaluable services of Alexander Campbell as a preacher of the Gospel, contributed in another way to the efficiency of his labors. After the rescue from shipwreck, and before the effects of the family could be put in readiness for a renewal of the voyage, the season had so far advanced as to make it impracticable to brave the dangers of the winter's storms. So it was decided to pass the winter in Scotland. This disappointment, keen as it was to the family of pilgrims, was an important factor in Alexander's preparation for the work to which he had recently dedicated his life. It needed the touch of a trained mind to perform the task for which Providence was fashioning him. So, this seeming calamity was now to prove a blessing in opening up the way to the long-deferred university studies, and an important event in the train of circumstances which contributed to his equipment for the work of the ministry.

As the father had seen university life at Glasgow, Alexander determined to spend the next few months within the shadow of the same venerable institution. So the family at once moved to Glasgow, and were soon settled within reach of the university.

Here Alexander, with his unquenchable thirst for knowledge, bent all the energies of his great mind in the mastery of such studies as would best fit him to preach the Word of Life. His student life, though of short duration, was one of intense mental activity. The habits of industry and early rising formed in youth now served him to good purpose. It was his custom to begin his work at four o'clock, and not to lay aside his books until ten at night. By an economical use of time, he was enabled, not only to keep in the front rank of his classes, but to do a vast amount of general reading. The list of books read during his one winter in Glasgow, of which he kept a memorandum, and from which he made copious extracts in his commonplace book, included poetry, ethics, natural history, philosophy, theology—in fact seemed to cover the whole range of moral and philosophical investigation. Such was his capacity for work, that in addition to his studies he managed to largely defray his expenses by teaching private classes in Latin, grammar, and arithmetic.

Another marked characteristic of his student life was his punctuality. He was never late at class. At every roll call he was on hand to respond, as the custom then was, with *ad sum*. It is related that some of the students, observing his habit, formed a plot to prevent him from entering the class-room until after the roll was called. Rushing upon him at the ringing of the bell, they seized him and attempted to hold him back until his name was passed. But, anticipating their purpose, with almost herculean strength, he shook them off, rushed up the college steps, and entered the class-room door just as his name was called.

While engaged in his studies at Glasgow, Alexander was brought under religious influences that were ultimately to change the whole cast of his theology, and which proved the final stage in the preparation of the young man for his work.

At a much earlier period his mind was awakened to some of the evils of sectarianism. One of the first subjects that attracted his attention after his conversion was the history of the church. His mind, as he read, was filled with wonder at the strange fortunes of Christianity; and what surprised him most of all was the numerous divisions into which religious society had broken. From the beginning he had been a keen observer of men and things, and that power he now used in the study of denominationalism. The first to claim his attention and stir within him a feeling of abhorrence was the Church of Rome with its superstitions, its ceremonials, its spiritual despotisms. That feeling he continued to cherish through life, regarding the Papacy as the bitterest foe of Gospel triumph. But when he turned from the dark chapter of Roman corruption and tyranny to the study of Protestantism, the spectacle was far from inviting. Instead of presenting a united front to its dangerous foe, it was rent into helpless fragments. Party-spirit reigned supreme. Denominations, almost without number, had been built on the most trivial differences. Even the Presbyterian Church, to one branch of which he belonged, had separated into numerous divisions,—National Church, Seceders, Burghers, Anti-Burghers, Old-Lights, New-Lights, etc.— thus checking the progress of truth and filling the religious world with confusion. All this, even at an early stage of his religious development, he regarded with the greatest antipathy, a feeling which was shared by his pious father.

It was, however, the cherished desire of Thomas Campbell that his son should become a minister in the branch of the Seceder Church to which he belonged. And as yet Alexander had no thought of pursuing any other course. Brought up in the most rigid Calvinistic school, it was no easy task to abandon all that he had learned, in exchange for what he ultimately came to believe to be the teaching of the Word of God. So, while pained at the bitterness of the religious strife about him, he had entered the University of Glasgow with no other purpose than the newly-formed one of preparing himself for the ministry of the Presbyterian Church. But the religious atmosphere of Glasgow began at once to exert a modifying influence upon his views, and was destined to work an entire revolution in his convictions and feelings with respect to existing denominations. In after years, in explaining his course, he declared that he had "imbibed disgust at the popular schemes, chiefly while a student at Glasgow."

Among the circumstances which contributed to this change was his meeting with Grenville Ewing, pastor of an Independent Church in Glasgow, to whom he brought a letter of introduction. This meeting was a fortunate one for the young student. An acquaintance sprang up between them which ripened into intimacy, and which brought Alexander into touch with a group of earnest men, who were at that time making themselves felt as a religious power, not only in Glasgow, but throughout Scotland. Taking a deep interest in young Campbell, Mr. Ewing often invited him to tea at his home. On these pleasant occasions he frequently met Robert and James Haldane, two brothers of wealth and influence, who were devoting their fortunes to the establishment of a better religious condition in Scotland.

In their zeal for the revival of the Lord's work, these brothers began to search the Word of God for a remedy for the religious deadness of the times. They soon discovered a wide discrepancy between the religious practices of the churches of their acquaintance and that authorized by the Scriptures. Believing this to be the chief cause of religious dearth, they became the heralds of a return to the Gospel requirements. The deep earnestness of their purpose is seen in the surrender which they made of their worldly ambition and fortune. The elder, Robert, arose from the study of his Bible declaring, "Christianity is everything or nothing. If it be true, it warrants and commands every sacrifice to promote its influence." From that time he, together with his brother, became the leader of a movement to reform the church and quicken a new religious interest in society. As evidence of acceptance with God, they preached the necessity of faith in his Son, rather than dependence on emotions, which men were taught to regard as assurances of salvation. Everywhere this movement, which for a time spread rapidly, was characterized by renewed devotion to the Scriptures; and many changes were made from existing practices in order to bring their obedience into closer conformity to the New Testament model. For example, while the Scottish Church celebrated the Lord's Supper only twice a year, Mr. Ewing was the first to introduce the custom of celebrating it every Lord's day, as more in harmony with the Scriptures. Later still, this movement led its adherents to abandon infant baptism as unscriptural, and finally to submit to immersion as the only authorized form of baptism.

While Alexander was in the midst of his studies, this agitation was at its height; and his warm friendship for its chief promoters caused him the more earnestly to investigate the truth of their claims. Cherishing as he did the feeling of religious unrest, he listened the more readily to men, who, like himself, were longing for some better way than the old beaten paths of tradition. Though not as yet accepting their peculiar views, a profound impression was made upon his mind, and the defense of the principles which they advocated, in a modified form, was destined to become the ruling passion of his life and ministry.

At last his doubts led him to question his right to continue in the fellowship of the Seceder Church. The crucial hour came at the semi-annual communion service, near the close of his sojourn in Glasgow. It was the custom to supply all who, according to the rules of the church, were entitled to a place at the Lord's Supper, with a metallic token, thus shutting out those deemed unworthy of this solemn privilege. Though filled with conscientious misgivings about sanctioning a religious system which he no longer approved, he finally decided to apply for a token. As he had no letter of recommendation from his home church in Ireland, it was necessary for him to pass an examination on the previous Saturday before the elders. This he did to the satisfaction of all. But when the hour for the celebration of the Lord's Supper arrived, his scruples overcame him, and instead of taking his place among the communicants, he cast his token into the plate that was passed around, and declined to partake with the rest. The ring of that token, as it fell from his hands, like the ring of Martin Luther's hammer on the door of the Wittenberg cathedral, announced his renunciation of the old church ties, and marks the moment at which he forever ceased to recognize the claims or authority of a human creed to bind upon men the conditions of their acceptance with God. Henceforth, he resolved, with the help of God, to stand for the defense of "the faith which was once delivered unto the saints."

While this evolution was going on in the heart of Alexander Campbell, the university session closed, and with it his college career. Though his course at the university was a short one, covering less than a year, he left it with a well- stored mind, and with powers trained for that keen logical discrimination which in later years contributed to his fame as a reasoner and debater.

Spring was now well advanced, but as there was no prospect of obtaining a suitable vessel for America for some time, he accepted the position of tutor to the young people of a number of families, who were spending the summer at a watering-place near Glasgow. Here, "freed from the routine and confinement of the college course, he spent some time very delightfully, in the midst of a highly cultivated and refined society," regretting only that the social and other duties of his position left him little time for reading and study.

Chapter Three:
EMIGRATION TO AMERICA

Two years and more had passed since the departure of Thomas Campbell for America, when the other members of the family were, on August 3, 1809, at last permitted to embark on the voyage which was to bring them together. We have seen how those years were spent by Alexander in diligent preparation for his future life-work. Leaving him to pursue the long and trying ocean voyage, let us see what the father had been doing in that time.

While Alexander Campbell's religious convictions were being remodeled by the influences at work at Glasgow, events were shaping themselves, under his father's ministry, for the exercise of his great gifts. New ideas demanded new soil. The fixed and conservative conditions of old-world society were inhospitable to new truths. The movement of the Haldanes and Ewings, which, as we have seen, led Alexander into new ways of thinking, ultimately failed of results, save as it imparted vitality to the existing religious order.

A new field awaited this fearless young champion of truth across the sea. Amidst the unsettled social conditions of America, a soil was being prepared for the planting. Thomas Campbell, on his arrival in Western Pennsylvania in 1807, at once found a promising field of labor among the hardy pioneers who had preceded him, and was soon recognized as a man of extraordinary power of heart and mind. But he was not long in discovering that, though he breathed the air of political freedom, the old spirit of religious intolerance and sectarian bigotry from which he fled prevailed even here. He was pained to find the party spirit of Christian society even more hostile and bitter than it had been in the neighborhood of his early ministry. In his zeal for Christian triumph he felt it to be his mission to attempt the correction of this disorder by infusing into the church to which he now ministered his own broad spirit of philanthropy and Christian fellowship.

Notwithstanding the sparsely settled condition of Western

Pennsylvania at that time, Thomas Campbell found the representatives of various religious bodies striving to keep up their separate organizations, each drawing the lines of fellowship closely about them, shutting out from the service and communion of Christ all who were not able to pronounce their party shibboleths. He was especially grieved to find that this was true of his own Presbyterian brethren.

The old contention between Burgher and Anti-Burgher, even on soil where the cause of their contention was removed,[1] continued to engender bitterness, each party denying to the other the ordinary privileges of Christian society. Other religious parties were not more charitable. In this way many an isolated family in the newly and thinly settled country, though deeply earnest in their Christian devotion, were deprived of Christian fellowship and even of the precious privilege of remembering their Lord's death in his memorial supper.

So generous were his own Christian sympathies, that Thomas Campbell determined to do what he could to remedy these evils, and bring what consolation was in his power to the lonely pioneers who felt their greatest sacrifice to be the loss of religious privileges which had been theirs in the old home-church elsewhere.

An opportunity soon presented itself for a practical application of his cherished views on the unity of Christ's followers. He was sent to minister to a few scattered brethren who were living some distance up the Alleghany, and to hold among them a communion service. Drawn together by his preaching were several families who had been members of other branches of the Presbyterian Church. His great heart was aroused with sympathy for these who were "as sheep without a shepherd." Many of them had not enjoyed the privilege of the Lord's Supper for a long time. In his preparation sermon he lamented the existing divisions of the church, and, feeling it his duty to exercise as broad a charity as he preached, he closed by inviting

---

[1] This division arose over the question whether certain oaths required by the burgesses of towns in Scotland were not unlawful, those favoring the oath being called Burghers, the opposing party Anti-Burghers.

all his pious hearers who were so disposed, irrespective of party differences, to join in the enjoyment of the communion season near at hand. For this act of liberality Mr. Campbell was speedily called to account. A young minister who had witnessed his unprecedented procedure hastened to prefer charges against him at the next meeting of the Presbytery, on the ground that he had failed to adhere to the standards and usages of the church. After an investigation, which called from him a most earnest plea in behalf of Christian liberty and fraternity, he was found deserving of censure. In vain did Mr. Campbell protest against the treatment he had received at the hands of his brethren. In vain did he appeal from Presbytery to Synod. Party spirit was unyielding. He had expressed sentiments, it insisted, which were "very different from sentiments held and professed by the church." This, it held, was an altogether sufficient ground of censure. From that time many of his fellow ministers became inimical to him, and were disposed to inflict on him at every opportunity their petty persecutions. Speaking to his son afterward of these trials, and of the jealousy and animosity that were now continually manifested toward him, he expressed it as his sincere conviction that "nothing but the law of the land had kept his head upon his shoulders."

At first Thomas Campbell, moved by a sense of loyalty to the church, submitted to the decision of his brethren, though insisting that his submission must not be regarded as a change of sentiment on his part, but merely an act of deference. After this concession he hoped that he would be permitted to continue his labors in peace. But, much to his regret, the hostility of his opponents continued. Misrepresentation, calumny, anything that would detract from his influence, were employed against him. Spies were employed to attend his meetings, so that, if possible, they might find fresh ground of accusation in his utterances. At last, worn out with these efforts, and having satisfied himself that corruption, bigotry, and tyranny were inherent in existing clerical organizations, he decided to sever his connection with the religious body to which he had given life-long support, renouncing the authority of the Presbytery and Synod, and announcing his abandonment of all these organizations.

By a strange coincidence, not long after this withdrawal of Thomas Campbell from the fellowship of the Seceder Church in Western Pennsylvania, his son, Alexander, without knowledge of his father's course, read himself out of the Presbyterian Church at Glasgow, by casting his metallic token in the plate, refusing by this act to sanction a system which he felt to be antagonistic to the spirit of Christ's prayer for the unity of his followers. Thus father and son, though separated by thousands of miles, had apparently acted in spiritual unison, and now found themselves in the anomalous attitude of servants of Christ without a church in which to serve him. But in withdrawing from the Seceders, it was no more a part of Thomas Campbell's plan to cease preaching the Word, than it was that of his son to abandon the work to which he had recently dedicated his life.

These painful experiences of Thomas Campbell soon led to important consequences. By his forced withdrawal from the Presbytery of the Seceders, he found himself without church affiliations. But that did not prevent him from continuing to preach Christ, or from seeking the extension of his kingdom. It only quickened his zeal in the cause that had always been near his heart: the union of Christ's followers in the bonds of a great fellowship and the end of the unseemly strife that had caused him constant pain.

He at once called together a company of friends, who, through his great personal influence, had become devotedly attached to him, and continued to preach to them the Word of Life. As the doors of the churches in which he formerly ministered were now closed against him, he was compelled to accept such accommodations as presented themselves. When the weather permitted he would gather his audiences beneath the shelter of a grove; but generally the houses of his old Irish neighbors were selected as the meeting place of those who were drawn together by the force of his plea for Christian liberality and Christian union. In these labors it was no part of his plan to organize a separate religious party. Such parties were already too numerous. At first he seems to have had no definite plan of action. He had simply determined to use his strength in such ways as Providence should open to him, in putting an end to partyism, by inducing the different denominations to unite together on the Bible. In this purpose many of his neighbors heartily sympathized with him, though as yet shrinking from the conclusions to which they were being irresistibly driven.

At last the times seemed ripe for some forward movement. Thomas Campbell proposed a special meeting, in which some formal statement of the principles he had been advocating might be made, and the movement given a wider consideration. A day was consequently named, and at the appointed time a large company assembled in an old farm-house in the neighborhood. The company was composed of thoughtful men, deeply conscious of the importance of the occasion. They did not bear credentials of great religious establishments to legislate for the church, or to invent tests of orthodoxy. And yet it may be doubted whether our country has witnessed a more important religious gathering. They were plain, hard-working pioneers, but they were men of faith, whose hearts were pained at the divided state of the church. Though belonging to different religious parties, they had met to seek a pathway to closer fellowship.

A feeling of deep solemnity pervaded the entire assembly, when, at length, Thomas Campbell arose to address them. The theme of the occasion had grown to be the burden of his heart. It was, therefore, with unusual force that he dwelt upon the manifold evils of a divided Christendom, and claimed for the Bible the right of determining the basis of Christian union. He closed this remarkable address with that famous declaration, which has since become the watchword of the Disciples of Christ: "Where the Scriptures speak, we speak; where the Scriptures are silent, we are silent."

It is said that upon the declaration of this principle a solemn silence followed. Then a Scotch Seceder, Andrew Munro, arose and said: "If we adopt that as a basis, then there is an end of infant baptism." Another became so affected by the consequences involved, that he burst into tears, after uttering a protest, and left the house. All felt that they had reached a crisis in their religious history. The assembly dispersed without any decisive action, but it had witnessed the birth-hour of an important movement. From this moment must be dated the "formal and actual commencement of the reformation," which has since been carried forward with so large a measure of success.

This important meeting was followed by another, on August 17, 1809, at which an organization was formed for the purpose of more effectually carrying out the principles to which its members had now become devoted. They called themselves "The Christian Association of Washington," and selected a committee of twenty-one to confer together with reference to some definite plan of action. To Thomas Campbell was entrusted the work of drawing up articles of agreement. These he was able to present at a meeting of his brethren, Sept. 7, under the title of *A Declaration and Address*.[1] This document bears so important a relation to the work inaugurated by Thomas Campbell and his illustrious son, that it deserves careful study. Omitting the greater portion of the preamble, the Declaration, submitted for the approval of those pioneer reformers, was as follows:

> *Our desire for ourselves and our brethren would be, that, rejecting human opinions and the inventions of men as of any authority, or as having any place in the church of God, we might forever cease from further contentions about such things; returning to and holding fast by the original standard; taking the Divine Word alone for our rule; the Holy Spirit for our teacher and guide, to lead us into all truth; and Christ alone, as exhibited in the word, for our salvation; that by so doing, we may be at peace among ourselves, follow peace with all men, and holiness, without which no man shall see the Lord. Impressed with these sentiments we have resolved as follows:*
>
> *1. That we form ourselves into a religious association under the denomination of the Christian Asso-*

---

[1] The *Declaration and Address* can be found in full in *Historical Documents Advocating Christian Unity*, compiled by Charles A. Young.

*ciation of Washington, for the sole purpose of pro-
moting simple evangelical Christianity, free from all
mixture of human opinions and inventions of men.*

*2. That each member, according to ability, cheer-
fully and liberally subscribe a certain specified sum to
be paid half-yearly, for the purpose of raising a fund
to support a pure Gospel ministry, that shall reduce to
practice that whole form of doctrine, worship, discipline, and government, expressly revealed and enjoined in the Word of God; and also for supplying the
poor with the Holy Scriptures.*

*3. That this society considers it a duty and shall use
all proper means in its power to encourage the formation of similar associations; and shall for this
purpose hold itself in readiness, upon application, to
correspond with, and render all possible assistance
to, such as may desire to associate for the same desirable and important purposes.*

*4. That this society by no means considers itself a
church, nor does at all assume to itself the powers
peculiar to such a society, nor do the members, as
such, consider themselves as standing connected in
that relation, nor as at all associated for the peculiar
purposes of church association, but merely as volun-
tary advocates for church reformation; and as pos-
sessing the powers common to all individuals, who
may please to associate in a peaceable, orderly
manner, for any lawful purpose, namely, the disposal
of their time, counsel and property, as they may see
cause.*

*5. That this society, formed fully for the sole pur-
pose of prompting simple, evangelical Christianity,
shall, to the utmost of its power, countenance and
support such ministers, and such only, as exhibit a
manifest conformity to the original standard in conversation and doctrine, in zeal and diligence; only
such as reduce to practice that simple, original form
of Christianity, expressly exhibited upon the sacred*

page; without attempting to inculcate anything of human authority, of private opinion, or inventions of men, as having any place in the constitution, faith, or worship of the Christian Church, or anything as of Christian faith or duty, for which there cannot be expressly produced a "Thus saith the Lord," either in express terms, or by approved precedent.[1]

Other resolutions, regulating the organization and fixing the time of the association meetings were added. This declaration was followed by a lengthy address in which were more fully stated and developed the principles of the movement, the whole, when put in type, filling fifty-four closely printed pages. This important document was at once adopted as the constitution of the association, and became the Magna Charta of the new religious movement now in its infancy. When we take into consideration the slavish subjection to customs and traditions which characterized the times, this is, in many respects, one of the most remarkable uninspired statements that religious history has produced.

While these events of deep religious importance were transpiring in Western Pennsylvania, word was brought Thomas Campbell that his family had landed in New York. Putting a copy of the newly-adopted address in his pocket, he hastened overland to meet them in their tedious journey by wagon across the country. It was his deep concern that his son be made acquainted with, and share in, the work that now engaged his attention; but he was somewhat anxious lest his new attitude should disturb the perfect sympathy which had hitherto characterized their relationship.

In the meantime, Alexander, as he pursued his slow journey over the mountains, most of the way on foot, was not a little disturbed at the possible consequences of the meeting. He had not had the courage to write his father of his withdrawal from the old church, and now feared lest his changed course would bring him pain. In this attitude of mind the meeting between

---

[1] *Memoirs of Alexander Campbell*, Vol. 1, page 243.

father and family occurred on the highway, some three or four days' journey from the new home. It was natural that, after the first fond greetings, two such spirits as Thomas Campbell and his son would find opportunity to consider hose weightier matters which pertained to their spiritual welfare. Happy was the surprise of both, when each learned that the other no longer adhered to the old religious party in which they had been reared. Alexander, who was ever conscious of the guiding hand of a higher Power, could not but admire the ways of Providence, which had, through bitter experiences, delivered each from the shackles of creed, so that instead of painful differences, they found themselves in perfect sympathy and accord.

It is fitting in this connection, after having observed the inauguration of the movement toward Christian union in Western Pennsylvania, to note, briefly, other conditions which greeted Alexander Campbell on his arrival in America, and contributed to the fruitfulness of the soil he was to cultivate.

The opening years of the century witnessed a great revival, which, notwithstanding the hindrances presented by sectarian bitterness, swept over the entire country. The country had suddenly awakened from the deadening influence of skepticism which followed the French Revolution, and men were everywhere seeking for the old faith, which, in their mad delusion, they had abandoned. In this frame of mind they were ready to investigate whatever promised to bring them into closer fellowship with God. About the same time the Total Abstinence Society began its work, greatly adding to the moral power of the church, by cleansing it of the blighting curse of drunkenness, and laying the foundation of an era of temperance reform, which has since proved the most useful handmaiden of the church in the work of human redemption. During the very month that Alexander Campbell landed at New York, four young men of Williams and Andover met together to dedicate themselves to the work of foreign missions, inaugurating the new missionary era, and becoming the forerunners of an army of Christian heroes, who have since planted the cross of Christ in every pagan land.

On this new and rising wave of religious feeling came this

young prophet of God, commissioned to speak burning words against the bitter hatred of sectarianism, and to call men's attention to the old landmarks which had been hidden beneath the theological rubbish of centuries. The field was ripe, and the laborer, equal to the task of the reaping, was at hand.

Chapter Four:
MINISTERIAL PREPARATION

Thomas Campbell had provided a home, such as the newly-settled country afforded, in the village of Washington, where the family circle was now happily reunited. Here a new world opened before the vision of Alexander. Western Pennsylvania was at that time the West, and its life and society were fashioned largely after the type of its wild and uncultivated surroundings; for those sturdy pioneers had little time or disposition to consider or cultivate the amenities of life. The study of these new conditions afforded for his inquisitive mind an agreeable occupation, and the spirit of liberty which was manifest on every hand accorded with his own independence of character.

These observations and studies were, however, not allowed to interfere with the more serious work of completing his preparation for the ministry. His studies, thus far, had been of those subjects which were intended to contribute to his mental discipline, without special reference to his life work. He had known the Scriptures from his youth, but he felt the need of a more thorough acquaintance with the Word of God, which he had now determined should be his only rule of life. So the first year in the new home was devoted to a most conscientious study of the Scriptures, with the view of efficiently presenting them to his fellowmen. These studies, as those of earlier years, were under the direction of his father, who, in lieu of a theological course, advised his son to "divest himself of all earthly concern, to retire to his chamber, to take up the Divine Book, and to make it the subject of his study for at least six months." In response to this wise counsel we discover him zealously pursuing his studies, broadening and deepening his knowledge of the truth, which was henceforth to furnish him the weapon of his warfare. The elder Campbell was now so occupied with his endeavors to promote the cause of union among the people, that he was necessarily absent from home much of the time, and Alexander was consequently thrown back upon his own resources. Long disciplined, however, in the school of self-education, he had no difficulty in meeting the situation before him; and in drinking from the stream that flowed pure and fresh from the fountain of Divine wisdom, gained, what the best theological course of the times could not have given him, an unbiased acquaintance with the Christian Scriptures.

Every moment of time, now, as at Glasgow, was earnestly devoted to self-improvement. He had just entered upon his twenty-second year, strong, resolute and purposeful, and felt that the Master's business demanded haste. That he might better account for his time, he arranged for himself a plan of studies for the winter of 1810, to which he religiously adhered. This program, which may help some of our young readers to the better employment of neglected moments, we give just as he wrote it for his own guidance:

> *One hour to read Greek—from 8 to 9 in the morning.*
> *One hour to read Latin—from 11 to 12 in the morning.*
> *One half hour to Hebrew—between 12 and 1 P. M.*
> *Commit ten verses of the Scripture to memory each day, and read the same in the original languages with Henry and Scott's notes and practical observations. For this exercise I shall allow two hours. These exercises being intended for every day, will not be dispensed with. Other reading and studies as occasion may serve. These studies in all require four and a half hours. Church history and divers other studies are intended to constitute the principal part of my literary pursuits.*
>
> *May God in his great mercy afford me time, ability and inclination to attend to these intentions, and to his name may all the glory and honor redound, through Jesus Christ. Amen. Alexander Campbell, Sunday, Dec. 31, 1809.*[1]

---

[1] *Memoirs of Alexander Campbell,* vol. 1, page 278.

In addition to these arduous, self-imposed tasks, he assumed the responsibility, during the hours unappropriated by study, of directing the education of the younger members of the family, and in assisting Abraham Altars, a promising member of the Association, in his studies preparatory to the work of the ministry.

The coming of this remarkable young man into the community was not unobserved. That Alexander was possessed of extraordinary powers was soon discovered, and inviting fields of labor were repeatedly offered him. A lawyer from Pittsburg, having formed his acquaintance, was so favorably impressed with his attainments and ability, that he urged him to take charge of an academy, of which he was trustee, offering $1,000 a year for his services, at that time a most tempting salary. Alexander did not hesitate to decline this flattering offer, giving as his reason, unswerving loyalty to the principles advocated by his father, and his determination to use all his energies in promoting the proposed reformation. Inducements were also offered, as soon as it was known that he was preparing himself for the ministry, to have him identify himself with some particular branch of the church, which would assure him popularity and a liberal support. The lofty impulses of his nature were never better illustrated than by the rejection of all these overtures, to become the champion of a cause which he knew would, in all probability, provoke the hostility of religious parties and which promised him nothing of earthly recompense.

In the interval of preparation for his work he was, as we have noted, a keen observer of the new conditions of society which surrounded him, and he was far from being pleased with the results of his observations. Coming from one of the most intelligent portions of Ireland, accustomed to educated and refined society, he was often shocked at the rudeness and unwonted freedom of young people in their social intercourse, and especially at their want of education and culture. While the energy of the pioneer was so largely consumed in clearing away the forests, and subduing the wilderness, and providing for the bare necessities of life, Alexander felt that there were, nevertheless, possibilities within the reach of these hardy, well-meaning settlers, which were being neglected. A born reformer, he became convinced that the community needed social, as well as religious reformation, and determined to do what was in his power to correct the social follies of his new surroundings. An opportunity presented itself in an invitation to contribute to the columns of the *Reporter*, a weekly paper published in the village of Washington. A series of original essays followed from his pen, in which he sought to infuse his own lofty ideals into the hearts of the young people of the community. These appeared over the nom de plume "Clarinda," and though written in a somewhat playful, yet satirical vein, illustrate the deeply serious purpose of the young man, and that command of strong, effective words which made him an opponent to be feared in any conflict in which principle was involved.

A little later he undertook, through the columns of the same journal, the more serious task of educational reform. The town boasted of a small, struggling institution of learning. But to this student of the old world university, with its stately and time-honored customs, the western college seemed to smack too much of the coarse, rude conditions of the frontier, to achieve its end in the training of young men for a sphere of culture and refinement. He therefore sought by his fearless pen to awaken its faculty and students to a higher conception of the aims and purposes of true education. His attacks stirred up a fierce controversy, which ran through many numbers of the *Reporter*; but he enjoyed the satisfaction in the end of having vanquished all his opponents, and in later years received the thanks of the very men whom he then transfixed on his intellectual lance. In these exercises the young reformer was whetting his blade for future conflicts in which he was to engage, and was given a foretaste of future triumphs that awaited his voice and pen, when he should fully enter upon his great work.

Though Alexander Campbell's life had thus far been spent in the training of mind and heart for the great work of winning men to Christ, as yet his powers of public address had been untried. It was not a young people's age, and little inducement or encouragement was offered them in the exercise of spiritual gifts. It was their place to sit at the feet of their elders in silence, unless God should in some unmistakable manner assure them of a call to the ministry.

Thus, at twenty-two Alexander seems never to have taken even a humble part in the public worship of God's house. Youthfulness, distrust of his untried powers, and, perhaps most of all, his high ideals of the ministerial office, caused him to hesitate about entering the pulpit. His conceptions of the necessary qualifications of a minister, written in his journal while yet a student at Glasgow, show that from the beginning he had set before him a high standard. He then adopted these rules, by which he seems to have modeled himself in his future course as a preacher:

1. The preacher must be a man of piety, and one who has the instruction and salvation of mankind sincerely at heart.

2. A man of modest and simple manners, and in his public performance and general behavior must conduct himself so as to make his people sensible that he has their temporal and eternal welfare more at heart than anything else.

3. He must be well instructed in morality and religion, and in the original tongues in which the Scriptures are written, for without them he can hardly be qualified to explain Scripture or to teach religion and morality.

4. He must be such a proficient in his own language, as to be able to express every doctrine and precept with the utmost simplicity, and without anything in his diction either finical on the one hand, or vulgar on the other.

5. A sermon should be composed with regularity and unity of design, so that all its parts may have a mutual and natural connection, and it should not consist of many heads, neither should it be very long.

6. A sermon ought to be pronounced with gravity, modesty, and meekness, and so as to be distinctly heard by all the audience.

7. Let the preacher, therefore, accustom himself to articulate slowly and deliver the words with a distinct voice, and without artificial attitudes or motions or any other affectation.[1]

He had scarcely accomplished his six months of retirement and study before his father began to urge upon him the importance of entering at once upon the active duties of the ministry. The harvest was great; the laborers were few. Almost alone the voice of Thomas Campbell sounded a return to the Gospel standard, but everywhere it found a responsive echo in hearts that were longing to see a new and better dispensation of things. Calls were coming faster than he could respond, and he foresaw the need of just such talents as he believed his son to possess.

At length, with many misgivings, Alexander consented to assist his father at one of his appointments. This was in the early spring of 1810. The place of meeting was a private house. It was arranged that the father should deliver the principal address, and that after a short intermission Alexander should speak. At the appointed time, he arose and spoke briefly, but with an ease and power that inspired him with confidence. This first effort could scarcely be called a sermon. It was simply an earnest exhortation, yet it so pleased the anxious father that he was heard to say, half aloud, at the close of his son's remarks, "Very well."

Encouraged by his first humble effort, and at the urgent request of those who heard him, Alexander now consented to prepare and deliver a public discourse. An appointment was consequently made for him to address a meeting on July 15, at a grove a few miles distant from Washington. His neighbors, who had already discovered his promising abilities, gathered in large numbers to hear the first discourse of the youthful preacher. It was a trying hour. Many a young preacher, who in the end has achieved success, has gone down at the first trial, and retired in shame, only to come forth to renewed and successful effort,

---

[1] *Memoirs of Alexander Campbell*, Vol. 1, page 138.

after days of excruciating agony. But Alexander Campbell was no ordinary young man. Like Minerva, who stepped full-grown from the brain of Jove, he stepped upon the platform an accomplished speaker, a master of assemblies, already possessed with the power to sway men's hearts. As he arose to speak, his commanding figure, coupled with the bloom of youthfulness which colored his cheek, arrested the attention of his audience, and his clear, ringing voice and quiet earnestness held their interest to the end.

The text for the occasion was taken from the closing verses of the Sermon on the Mount, "Therefore, whosoever heareth these sayings of mine and doeth them, I will liken him unto a wise man, who built his house upon a rock." His purpose that day was in perfect accord with the message of the text. He had himself been sitting, in profound and wrapt attention, at the feet of the Master, and it had become his unalterable determination to hear the sayings of Christ and do them. Without pausing to consider in detail this sermon, an outline of which is preserved in his *Memoirs*, it is sufficient to note the impression made by it upon both the audience and the speaker.

The sermon had been prepared with great pains, as were all his early efforts, written in full and committed to memory, not a difficult task for one of his grasp of mind. It embodied the speaker's own deeper convictions of the truth. "There was something in the reverential bearing of the speaker, in the unaffected simplicity of his manner, in the appropriateness of his expressions, and in the earnest, distinct intonations of his clear, commanding voice, that seemed to rivet the attention of all upon the thought and the pictures he presented." Without attempting to play the orator, he had struck the keynote of persuasive art. As the young preacher closed his discourse, but one opinion prevailed. It was the universal judgment that he could preach better than his father, which, in view of the reputation of Thomas Campbell as a speaker, was the highest compliment they could bestow.

The effect of the discourse upon the speaker himself was not less marked than its impression upon the people. He had established his reputation among the members of the Association to which he belonged. He had done more. He had discovered Alexander Campbell to himself. To his great joy he realized that he had not mistaken his calling when he dedicated his life to the ministry of the Word, and it was his delight, henceforth, to exercise his gifts continually for the elevation of his fellowmen.

That he might escape the imputation of mercenary motives, and that he might be actuated in his course only by unselfish love for Christ, he had already decided to serve his Master without earthly reward, save that which comes from a consciousness of doing good. Announcing this determination to his father, the latter replied, "Upon these principles, my son, I fear you will have to wear many a ragged coat." He nevertheless strictly adhered to his purpose, refusing, during his entire ministry, to accept any remuneration for the preaching of the Gospel, and often, like Paul, laboring "with his own hands," to provide the temporal necessities.

Having demonstrated his power as a preacher, the services of Alexander Campbell were from this time in constant demand. The field, it is true, would not be regarded as an inviting one by the young preacher of today. No city congregations extended calls to him. No great churches opened their doors that he might enter. No metropolitan dailies opened their columns to reports of his sermons. His fame was as yet confined to the scattered pioneers of his own vicinity, and he gladly responded to their calls, content that a door of usefulness had opened to him. These early labors were carried on in the neighboring villages, in the farm-house, the spacious barn, or, when weather permitted, under the shade of some inviting grove. Wherever an opportunity presented itself, he went, and since he had ruled the matter of compensation out of the question, a congregation of poor farmers afforded him as promising a field as would a metropolitan temple with its capital and culture. Thus during the first year he preached more than one hundred sermons, in all these early efforts maintaining the standard he had set for himself, and adding to his local reputation as a preacher of extraordinary power.

A great help to the young preacher at this period was the

kindly criticism of his father. Thomas Campbell had been trained after the strict rules of the Scotch Seceder clergy, in the composition and arrangement of his sermons. Each effort was a model of homiletic exactness. These rules he was now disposed to apply for the improvement of his son. It was his invariable custom, after hearing his son preach in these early efforts, to test the sermon upon his return home by the established rules, or when the father preached the son was encouraged to do the same. The special point of this friendly criticism was that the division of the subject exhausted it, and that its doctrines were strictly those of the text. With such a mentor, Alexander was saved from the homiletic blunders into which young ministers so often fall.

Another event in the life of Alexander Campbell, which, while perhaps not strictly a part of ministerial preparation as prescribed by the Seminaries, had such a vital bearing upon his life-work that it very properly presents itself for consideration in this connection. He had now arrived at an age when his thoughts turned upon another subject of vital importance to human welfare and happiness. He believed with the Scriptures that it was not good for man to be alone. Along with his great intellectual power, he had a warm domestic nature that sought and found its keenest enjoyment in the home circle. But, if up to this period he had seriously contemplated a matrimonial alliance, his biographer has not mentioned it. Indeed, from his letters published in the *Weekly Reporter*, to which allusion has already been made, he seems to have taken unromantic views of the question, frowning upon the unusual liberties exercised by the young people of his community, and condemning with all the earnestness of his nature the matrimonial yoke too carelessly assumed.

To him life was full of great problems, and the choosing of a wife who was to share in their solution was not the least serious business before him. His character was altogether too well-balanced for his heart to run away with his head, or to be led into any alliance which would not further him in the great mission of his life.

The circumstances which led to his marriage are unromantic in the extreme. His father, in his ministry to the scattered saints, had formed the acquaintance of John Brown, an intelligent and prosperous farmer across the State line, in what is now West Virginia. As Thomas Campbell's labors frequently brought him into the neighborhood, this acquaintance ripened into a warm friendship. They were akin in their deep interest in religious themes and in their literary tastes. During one of his visits, Thomas Campbell promised Mr. Brown some favorite books, and upon his return to Washington sent them down by his son Alexander. This errand was destined to be an important one in his career. In the family of Mr. Brown was an only daughter, Margaret, then some eighteen years of age, whom he now for the first time met. She is described as tall, slender, and graceful, with a sweet, benignant countenance and most engaging manners. Nor was she deficient in those graces of mind and heart which give to beauty its real charm. She was noted in the neighborhood for her piety and industry; and had enjoyed the best educational privileges at that time provided for young women. On the whole, her warm, gentle nature was suited to the strong, rugged intellect of the young preacher, and he was not long in discovering it. He found it easy to invent or discover excuses for repeating his visits. His talents and acquirements soon won for him a hearty welcome in the family circle, and his sprightly and agreeable conversational powers made him a most enjoyable companion. The intimacy thus established between Alexander Campbell and the Brown family led to warmer feelings between the daughter and himself, which ended in a proposal of marriage, and their union on March 12, 1811.

Following his marriage, Mr. Campbell went to live with his father-in-law; and while continuing to preach at different points within the reach of his new home his delight in active exercise led him at once to engage in assisting Mr. Brown in the management of the farm. Having acquired a practical knowledge of farming in boyhood, he entered upon his new duties with the ability and zeal that characterized all his undertakings.

Here he also displayed his extraordinary capacity for achievement, combining with his daily labors on the farm an uninterrupted study of the great questions that concerned him as a minister of the Gospel. Physical exercise seemed only to whet his mind to a keener edge; and his enjoyment of outdoor life was not allowed to interfere with the regular course of study which he continued to prescribe for himself. As an illustration of his method of study, we give the following instance: "When his horses, weary with the plow, were resting for a little while in the shade, he would take from his pocket the New Testament he always carried, and spend the time in committing a portion of it to memory, or in tracing out the order and method of a discourse upon some important theme."[1] He continued to observe the old habit, formed during his student life, of early rising, and thus gained many a quiet hour for study while others slept. The noon-hour, too, while resting from labor, was similarly occupied. He thus spent every moment, disengaged from labor, either in study or in conversing about the great subjects amidst which he continually dwelt. In a carefully preserved catalogue he kept a list of all the books he read, and a summary of all the important truths they contained; and during the first year of his married life he read, according to his own estimate, thirty-five volumes, containing an aggregate of 8,354 pages. Nor were these read in a superficial manner, but with the greatest care, making extensive extracts of such portions as he desired to remember.

Thus in an obscure corner of the earth, and in humble occupations, Providence was fashioning the mind and heart of a religious leader, who was shortly, like John the Baptist in the wilderness of Judea, to unmask the pharisaism of his time, and to call a world of erring ecclesiasts to true repentance.

---

[1] *Memoirs of Alexander Campbell*, Vol. 1, page 441.

Chapter Five:
RELIGIOUS DISCOVERIES

About the time of Alexander Campbell's marriage, a crisis came to the affairs of the Christian Association. The nucleus of friends who gathered about him and his venerable father, began insensibly to assume the position of a distinct religious body. This awakened the deep concern of the elder Campbell. It had never been his intention to add to the confusion of the religious world by founding or encouraging a separate religious society. From the first he had insisted that the Association was in no sense to be regarded as a church. It was merely to be an organization of men, working through the various churches to which they belonged, for the union of God's children.

It had been a matter of continuous regret to Thomas Campbell that he had been compelled to withdraw for a season from the church that nurtured him; and now he shrank from the responsibility of creating a new religious party, and was disposed to the adoption of any measure by which such a result could be avoided. Foreseeing the danger, he was led, some months previous, through the suggestion of friends in the Presbyterian Church, to consider favorably an ecclesiastical union with that body. Why should he not? His own forgiving nature had refused to cherish resentment for the treatment accorded him by his brethren. As yet he and most of his followers held, in the main, to the doctrines of the Westminster Confession of Faith. The only alternative was the organization of an independent church. Influenced by a strong desire to conserve the peace of religious society, he finally concluded to apply for membership in the Presbyterian Synod, soon to meet in Washington. His son, with keener foresight, did not anticipate any favorable result, but acceded to his father's plans.

Accordingly Thomas Campbell appeared before the Synod, explaining the principles of the Association to which he belonged, and asking admission for himself and his brethren. His friendly overtures were rejected, and his reception into "ministerial and Christian communion" denied on the vague claim that there were "important reasons" for this decision. Stung by this denial, and its implied reflection upon his own ministerial standing, he demanded to know what the "important reasons" were. He was informed that the most serious were his attitude of indifference toward infant baptism, his opposition to creeds and confessions, and the encouragement which he had given his son to preach the Gospel without any regular authority. These were the grounds of his offending, and not any irregularity of life or conduct on his part. No concessions which he could conscientiously make would remove these barriers, though he humbly promised to be obedient to the Synod in everything, if only he were permitted to advocate "Christian union upon Christian principles." This privilege he could not and would not surrender, and the Presbyterian fold was not then large enough to admit him on such a platform.

Upon the failure of this well-meant effort, nothing remained for the members of the Association, in their desire for church-fellow- ship, but to resolve themselves into an independent church. Thomas Campbell, with great reluctance, finally gave his consent that steps should be taken to effect such an organization, and a meeting for this purpose was appointed for May 4, 1811. At this meeting it was proposed that admission to membership should be granted to those who gave satisfactory answer to the question, "What is the meritorious cause of a sinner's acceptance with God?" To this test question, which was never again propounded, thirty gave satisfactory answers, and were enrolled as the members of the new church. Thomas Campbell, the originator and leader of the movement, was selected as the elder, four deacons were chosen, and Alexander Campbell, whose great talents were now recognized, was licensed to preach the Gospel.

Thus was formally organized a distinct religious communion, known as the Brush Run Church, a veritable church in the wilderness. These thirty valiant names, banded together in the search for, and in the common pursuit of, a more excellent way of Christian conquest than that presented by the strife and bitterness of sectarianism, formed a new band of Pilgrim Fathers, before whom was an unbeaten path and many perils. But right heroically did they pursue their way in the face of obstacles that to us seem almost insurmountable.

In many essential respects this pioneer church differed from the thousands of churches which have sprung from its foundation; but it had already caught the underlying truths which culminated in the principles today advocated by a great Christian brotherhood. Two vital principles constituted its platform. (1) The sole authority of the Bible as the basis of faith and fellowship. Thomas Campbell's famous declaration, "Where the Scriptures speak we speak; where the Scriptures are silent we are silent," made further statement of belief or terms of fellowship than those given in the Bible impossible. (2) The second principle was that which had consumed the life of Thomas Campbell: the exaltation of the standard of union in Christ. The new church was to be a beacon-light calling the attention of the world to the prayer of the Master that "they all may be one." Farther than this it did not, at this time, seem prepared to go. Its members had not even stopped to consider the logical conclusions to which their own principles would lead them. The plan of salvation, the form and meaning of baptism, and many other questions that were dividing the religious world, had not as yet claimed their serious attention. But the leaven had been planted, and would in time work out the fullness of the Master's purpose.

That the views of Alexander Campbell were in perfect accord with the main object of this newly organized church, we have evidence in his own utterances. "I dare not be a party man," said he, "for these reasons:

> *1. Because Christ has forbidden me. He has commanded us to keep the "unity of the Spirit;" to be "of one mind and of one judgment;" to "love each other with a pure heart fervently," and to "call no man master" on earth.*
>
> *2. Because no party will receive into communion all whom God would receive into heaven. God loves his children more than creeds, and man was not made for the Bible, but the Bible for man. But if I am asked*

by a partisan, Could you not join us and let these things alone? I answer, no, because—

3. The man that promotes the interest of a party stands next in guilt to the man that made it. The man that puts a second stone on a building is as instrumental in its erection as the man that laid the first. He that supports a party bids the party God speed; and he that bids them God speed is a partaker of their evil deeds.

4. Because all parties oppose reformation. They all pray for it; but they will not work for it. None of them dare return to the original standard. I speak not against any denomination in particular, but against all. I speak not against any system of truth, but against all except the Bible. "Hold fast the form of sound words" condemns them all. It is a doleful truth, that the very persons who ought to have advocated reformation, always opposed it.[1]

The first need of the new church was a meeting-place. Thus far the meetings had been held wherever opportunity afforded, generally in the houses of its devoted members. But the steps recently taken made a fixed meeting-place indispensable to the permanence and success of the movement. The members, therefore, set to work diligently in the construction of a rude building at Brush Run, and so rapidly was the work prosecuted by these willing hands, that by June 16, Alexander Campbell was able to preach the first sermon in the new meeting-house. So poor were most of the members that they were unable to finish the interior of this modest frame building, and assembled in it for worship even during the inclemency of winter without stoves or other appointments of comfort. But the chill and cheerlessness of their surroundings found compensation in the ardor of their devotion and the warmth of their affection which had been elevated above the love of party by the love of Christ.

An episode occurred at this first meeting which soon led to

---

[1] *Memoirs of Alexander Campbell*, Vol. 1, page 353.

important changes in the practice of this infant church. It was resolved that the Lord's Supper should be celebrated weekly, in conformity with the example of the primitive church; but at the first communion service it was observed that several who were regarded as members did not partake of the emblems. On inquiry, it was discovered that they did not consider themselves scriptural subjects, as they had not been baptized. Upon further inquiry, it was learned that they would be satisfied with nothing but immersion as scriptural baptism. Though Thomas Campbell had himself been sprinkled in infancy, and did not as yet question the validity of his baptism, he did not scruple to accede to the demands of these members, since they had never been baptized. So they were taken to a pool in Buffalo Creek, and with due ceremony immersed. It is curious to observe the manner of this first immersion in the new church, which would now scarcely be regarded as befitting the solemnity of the occasion. He requested the candidates to wade out into the pool, to the depth of their shoulders, while he climbed out on an overhanging root, and bent their heads beneath the water, repeating as he did so the baptismal formula. But whatever may have been thought of the manner in which the baptism was administered, it was significant that Thomas Campbell, the leader of this reformatory movement, should be the first to introduce immersion, a practice which has since become one of the distinguishing features of the Christian Church.

The early years following the organization of the Brush Run Church were eventful years in the history of the new movement. Its promoters had launched upon an untried sea, and had not yet learned their bearings. But they had an unfailing compass on board in the Word of God. Following its direction, they were being continually led toward the desired haven of Truth; but not without encountering many a storm of bitter opposition, and many perilous experiences.

Alexander Campbell, having cut loose from his old religious moorings, was now confronted by many difficult problems. The way seems so plain to us that we can scarcely conceive of the trials of those pioneer days. His early religious training, and the accepted customs of religious society, were barriers that intercepted the full flash of truth. But having now resolved to accept nothing upon the traditions of the fathers, he determined that each step before him should be taken under scriptural guidance, and not until he was clearly convinced that he was following in the footsteps of the Master. This accounts for the gradual unfolding of the principles of the new reformation, covering a period of some sixteen years, from 1811 to 1827.

Having first convinced himself of the scripturalness of his position, he was ordained to the ministry upon the recommendation of the Brush Run Church on the first day of the new year 1812. He had already, as we have seen, been doing acceptable work as a preacher, but he felt that the time had come that his life must be irrevocably dedicated to religious work. He did not regard the ceremony of ordination as conferring any authority which he did not already possess, but as a public testimony that the person ordained possessed the necessary authority.

As the result of a searching self-examination at this time, he has left us the following heart-picture of himself, in which he enumerates the Providential circumstances that made the humble office of the ministry his final and unalterable choice:

> *Special instances of Divine power, which I consider to bind me under obligations to be specially devoted to Him, with my whole mind, soul and body:*
>
> *1. In being born of religious parents, and of course religiously educated.*
>
> *2. In receiving an education, in some respects, to qualify me for that office, and this education providential in the following respects: (1) In my grand desire at first being not to preach the Gospel, but to shine in literary honors and affluence. (2) In my design being frustrated, and my mind turned to desire that office. (3) In my being introduced, quite contrary to expectation, to the University of Glasgow, and the literary advantages there.*
>
> *3. In resolving, when in imminent danger at sea, to serve God in this way, on two occasions of extraor-*

dinary deliverance.

4. In my situation being such upon my arrival in this country, that I could not prepare myself for any other office.

5. In the particular persecutions that befell my father, which shut up any prospects of support in the exercise of that office, yet in my giving it the preference.

6. In my favorable and easy circumstances for that purpose.

7. In giving me a choice companion, congenial to my inclination of serving Him.

8. In giving me some desire after his salvation.

9. In giving me some desire after the salvation and reformation of mankind.

10. In giving me tolerably good talents for edifying others.

11. In giving me a call from the church to preach the Gospel.

12. In my desire to suffer hardships and reproach in that good work.[1]

It was natural that one actuated by such high and disinterested motives should shrink from no step urged by the dictates of conscience and duty. In this we find the true spirit of a reformer, and many were the changes that it soon led him to make.

The question of scriptural baptism, to which he had hitherto given little attention, now came before him in new light. The arrival of a daughter in the new home made the question of infant baptism one of "immediate, practical interest." From his early education, he had come to look upon it as a religious act not to be neglected, but he now discovered to his satisfaction that it was without divine authority. But a more startling thought came to his mind while engaged in this investigation. If infant baptism was unscriptural, had he ever himself been bap-

---

[1] *Memoirs of Alexander Campbell,* Vol. 1, page 381.

tized? Previously he had put the question aside by saying, "As I am sure it is unscriptural to make this matter a term of communion, I let it slip. I wish to think and let think on those matters." But that answer no longer satisfied his conscience. He must know the mind of the Master. A careful study of the whole subject followed. Abandoning all uninspired authorities, he applied himself afresh to the study of the Bible.

At the conclusion of this investigation, he discovered that not only the baptism of infants, but its administration by sprinkling, was unauthorized, and that he was an unbaptized person. In this conclusion his wife heartily concurred, and both resolved to obey the command of Christ in the light of his Word. With him, to resolve was to act. Wishing to proceed without delay, he made application to Matthias Luce, a Baptist minister of his acquaintance, to perform the rite. Out of respect to his father, he thought best to acquaint him with his purpose. In the interview, Thomas Campbell was reticent, but offered no particular objection; and on the day appointed for baptism, to the surprise of all, appeared in readiness to yield similar obedience, along with wife and oldest daughter. The occasion was a memorable one. A large company of friends had assembled on the banks of the Buffalo, for, having become convinced of his duty, Alexander determined that the people to whom he preached should have the opportunity of witnessing this public profession of his former error.

At this point, Alexander Campbell took another step toward the restoration of the New Testament pattern. Hitherto believer's baptism had only been administered upon certain accepted tests of the spiritual fitness of the candidate, called a religious experience. Believing that the only divinely-authorized prerequisite to baptism was an acknowledgment of the Messiahship of Jesus, Mr. Campbell stipulated that he was to receive baptism on the simple confession that "Jesus is the Son of God," declaring, "I have set out to follow the apostles of Christ and their Master, and I will be baptized only into the primitive Christian faith."

This step taken by the leaders of the new movement, soon led to important changes that became far-reaching in their results.

The first was the change of position which Thomas and Alexander Campbell henceforth sustained to the movement. Up to this point Thomas Campbell had been the recognized and trusted leader. It was his voice that first sounded the call to God's wrangling children to cease from their unseemly strife. It was his pen that marked out a pathway to a broader and holier fellowship. But "from the moment Thomas Campbell concluded to follow the example of his son in relation to baptism." the mantle of leadership passed to the latter. Without rivalry or jealousy, and in the same perfect confidence and loving companionship, they continued to share the labors of the cause they had espoused, but it was Alexander who, henceforth, stood in the forefront, strong, resolute, aggressive, the recognized leader of the Reformation, intensely hated by his enemies, ardently admired and loved by his friends.

The course of Alexander Campbell and his father, relative to the question of baptism, was soon followed by a majority of the congregation, and in the end immersion was unanimously recognized as the only scriptural baptism.

Chapter Six:
TRIALS AND TRIUMPHS

As was to be expected, the attitude of the Brush Run Church in becoming a body of immersed believers, awakened a storm of opposition from the Pedo-baptist ranks, and its members became the subjects of no little persecution. Misrepresentations of all kinds were freely circulated among the people. Family and friendship ties were broken, and the common civilities of society were denied to this new order of heretics. It is related that Alexander Campbell, returning after nightfall from one of his appointments about this time, was overtaken by a violent storm. Calling at the home of a Seceder lady, he sought shelter. Before granting his request she desired to know his name. Being informed that it was Alexander Campbell who sought her hospitality, she promptly refused him admittance, giving as a reason her hostility to his religious views; so he was obliged to continue his journey in the face of a furious tempest, through an almost trackless forest, until he reached home.

These trials, so far from discouraging this feeble band of reformers, served rather to strengthen their faith and purpose. Convinced of the correctness of their course, they were drawn more closely to each other by the petty persecutions which they were now called to suffer. "They often visited each other's houses, often spending a considerable portion of the night in social prayer, in searching the Scriptures, asking and answering questions, and singing hymns of praise." Thus was laid, in obscurity and adversity, the foundation of a great religious movement.

A new situation now confronted Mr. Campbell and his followers. The course which brought them into disfavor with Pedo-baptists secured their acceptance with Baptists. Since they had become immersionists, the latter began to manifest a friendly interest in them, and urged them to become members of the Redstone Association, which embraced all the Baptist churches of that region. The matter was laid before the members of the Brush Run Church in the autumn of 1813. After much hesitation and prayerful consideration, it was decided to enter the Association, on condition that its members should be independent of all human creeds, and should enjoy the privilege of preaching whatever they learned from the Holy Scriptures, "regardless of any creed or formula in Christendom." Upon these terms they were received, and a union was formed which for several years furnished a home for this infant church.

Speaking of his religious views at this period, Mr. Campbell said: "I am now an Independent in church government and a Baptist in so far as respects baptism." While differing in many things from the views held by the Baptist ministers with whom he was associated, he was ready to grant that liberty of opinion which, had it been granted him in turn, might have led to a permanent and happy union in Christ's service.

In the meantime Mr. Campbell continued to preach in connection with his labors on the farm, but without making any decided impression on the community. Occasionally individuals presented themselves for baptism, but the loss by removals equaled the gains by accession, and the church was scarcely able to preserve its original number. Discouraged over the meager results of his labors, he favorably entertained a movement, now set on foot by some of his friends, to plant a religious colony in some unsettled portion of Ohio. It was urged that with a membership so scattered, nothing could be accomplished in the face of the opposition encountered, and that in a newer section of the country they could improve their condition and increase their usefulness. Mr. Campbell was invited to join the company, and was made a member of the committee sent out to select a suitable location.

After visiting different portions of the State, the vicinity of Zanesville was selected as the most suitable location for carrying out the purposes of the society, and it was decided that removal should take place as soon as they could individually make arrangements to do so.

In this new field it was felt that greater progress could be made in advocating the principles of the Christian Association. But this was not to be God's method in the promotion of his cause. When Mr. Campbell, on his return, acquainted his father-in-law with his intentions, Mr. Brown seriously opposed the project, objecting to the removal of his only daughter and his son-in-law, whom he regarded with great esteem, to so great a distance. As an inducement to keep them near him, he offered to present Mr. Campbell with the fine farm on which he lived. This generous offer Mr. Campbell gratefully accepted, abandoning the colonization scheme, which now fell through, and entering with new zeal upon his combined labors as farmer and preacher. By this gift he was providentially provided with the means which enabled him to devote his energies unreservedly and without remuneration to the spread of reformatory principles. His management of the farm which thus came into his possession, was with an industry and ability that did not fail to commend him to the neighboring farmers; but he never allowed these labors to interfere with his regular appointments for preaching, or to interrupt his communion with the great spirit of Truth.

Thus began the home to which Alexander Campbell, with his great nature, was always warmly attached, and to which, after his long campaigns of later years, he returned to find refreshing rest and his keenest enjoyment. For the home thus providentially furnished him on the "beautiful flowing Buffalo," became after a time his beloved Bethany, where he engaged in his intensest labors, and which deserves ever to be celebrated as the cradle of the Nineteenth Century Reformation.

The situation in which Mr. Campbell found himself, soon after his connection with the Redstone Association of the Baptist churches, was far from inviting. The originality of his method in dealing with the Scriptures, and his utter disregard for customs, however time-honored, which were not sanctioned by primitive precept or example, awakened the suspicion of the more narrow-minded of the Baptist ministers, who were not slow in manifesting their disapproval. His popularity among the churches of the Association, no doubt added to their displeasure, and at every opportunity he was made to feel the sting of their resentment.

This hostility, which at first manifested itself in slights and little annoyances, at last led to an open attack upon his teachings. In August, 1816, in spite of the intrigues of his enemies, he was invited to speak at the annual meeting of the Association. Upon this occasion he preached his memorable *Sermon on the Law*,[1] taking his text from Romans 8:3: "For what the law could not do, in that it was weak through the flesh, God sending his own Son in the likeness of sinful flesh, and for sin, condemned sin in the flesh." In this discourse, he made, for the first time, the distinction between the law and the Gospel, the old and the new dispensation, which afterward afforded him an impregnable position in his conflict with the religious errors of his time. A sentence or two from the conclusion of the discourse, which may be found in full in Mr. Campbell's published works, will reveal the high spiritual tone of his utterance:

> *The Christian dispensation is called the ministration of the Spirit, and, accordingly, everything in the salvation of the church is accomplished by the immediate energy of the Spirit. Jesus Christ taught his disciples that the testimony concerning himself was that only which the Spirit would use, in converting such of the human family as should be saved. He would not speak of himself, but what he knew of Christ. Now he was to convince the world of sin, of righteousness, of judgment, not by applying the law of Moses, but the facts concerning Christ, to the consciences of the people. The Spirit accompanying the words which the apostles preached, would convince the world of sin; not by the ten precepts, but because they believed not in him,—of righteousness, because he went to the Father,—and of judgment, because the prince of the world was judged by him. So that Christ, and not law, was the Alpha and Omega of their sermons, and this the Spirit made effectual to the salvation of thou-*

---

[1] The *Sermon on the Law* can be found in its entirety in *Historical Documents Advocating Christian Union*, as well as *Alexander Campbell: A Collection (Volume 2)*.

sands. [1]

While the sermon presented nothing but the plain Scripture teaching on the subject, it was so bold an assault upon the theology and preaching current among the Baptists at that time, that it created a profound sensation. The lay members were, for the most part, pleased with its simple, natural presentation of the truth, but it only added fuel to the flame of bitterness which some of his fellow-preachers cherished toward him. "This will never do," they said. "This is not our doctrine."

Mr. Campbell, in consequence of views presented in this sermon, was "brought up for trial and condemnation" at the next meeting of the Association, which was held in the autumn of 1817. At that time but few were ready to accept his advanced religious conclusions, the actual advocates of the Reformation, scattered among the Baptists of three States, not numbering more than one hundred and fifty persons. Notwithstanding this feeble support, upon investigation he was acquitted of the charges made against him, but the persecution and misrepresentation continued. His enemies employed every means within their power to create prejudice against him, and from that time until his withdrawal from the Association, charges of heresy were annually preferred.

The difficulties Mr. Campbell now encountered convinced him that he had nothing to hope from his brethren in the ministry, and that if his efforts at religious reformation were to succeed, it must be by the aid of young men trained under his direction. This led him to devote his energies for a time to the work of education.

From early manhood he had manifested a deep interest in everything that would contribute to the intellectual development of his fellowmen. At the age of seventeen he had entered the schoolroom as his father's assistant. Later, in his father's absence, he had assumed the management of the school. On his arrival in America he used his pen with effect in advocating a better method of instruction than that employed by the pioneer

---

[1] *Millennial Harbinger*, 1846.

educators of Western Pennsylvania. As now he worked out for himself a line of action in connection with the proposed religious reformation, he felt that its success demanded of its advocates the highest intellectual attainments possible. So deeply was he convinced of the need of an educated ministry, that he resolved at once to undertake the instruction of young men, if any could be found who should aid in the cause of primitive Christianity. Early in 1818 he set on foot an educational enterprise which he hoped would accomplish this object. At the beginning of this year he announced his purpose of opening a seminary in his own house, chiefly for young men, thus adding to his other labors the arduous one of an instructor. The project in one particular was remarkably successful; in another it was a failure.

The standing of his father as an educator, and his own reputation for energy and talent, soon brought him more pupils than he could accommodate. Not only from his own neighborhood, but from Pittsburg and other points more distant, young men came to enjoy the benefits of his scholarship. Those from a distance he boarded in his own family, and not only undertook the direction of their studies, but also sought to imbue their minds with a love for, and acquaintance with, the Scriptures, and to awaken a religious interest through the morning and evening devotions of his household.

It is curious to note the expense of an education in this backwoods seminary. The tuition for any of the branches commonly taught in academies, including Hebrew and French, was five dollars a quarter; while board and lodging were had for the modest sum of one dollar and a half per week. The discipline, too, was of a rather more vigorous type than that commonly employed in such institutions. Many of the young men were sent to him because they had been shut out of other schools on account of insubordination. These, Mr. Campbell took in charge with a vigorous hand, in one instance administering a severe flogging to the ring-leader, and establishing an authority that none henceforth dared question. But if he was at times severe, his genial nature, his warm sympathies, his winsome manner, and his inexhaustible fund of information, in the end, won the respect and friendship of all who came under his influence.

But while he succeeded beyond his expectation in the work of securing and disciplining young men, in one respect the school proved a great disappointment to him. He greatly desired to see some of his pupils consecrate themselves to the cause of truth, and join him in his crusade against religious error. It is not strange, when we consider the attitude of religious society toward Mr. Campbell at that time, that his desire was in no satisfactory measure realized. His views were regarded with suspicion, if not with bitter hostility. The acceptance of his cause promised nothing but reproach and persecution. It did not even hold out the prospect of moderate pecuniary support. Only minds stirred with the deepest convictions could be induced to enlist in such a cause, and it is not strange, in view of these conditions, that the young men under his instruction shrank from identifying themselves with so unpromising a movement.

The Buffalo Seminary, notwithstanding its failure to win ministerial recruits, was continued for several years. Finding the burdens heavy, in 1819 Mr. Campbell called his father to his assistance; but even then he found his strength inadequate to the task of keeping up the school in connection with the growing demands upon his time as a preacher of the reformation. His health began to suffer from confinement in the schoolroom, and since the school did not subserve the chief purpose for which it was established, he concluded to discontinue it. So this early educational enterprise ended its career in 1822.

The failure of Alexander Campbell's endeavors, and those of his father, to secure the adoption of reform principles within existing parties, for a time limited his aim, and caused him to despair of seeing any change in religious society. So far from assuming the position of a public reformer, he abandoned all expectation of more than the formation of a single congregation, with which he could enjoy the exercise of Gospel privileges, as he conceived them in the New Testament. But all this while he was accomplishing more than he dreamed of. The leaven was at work; and his own reputation, in spite of the efforts of his enemies to bring him into disrepute, was growing among the scattered Baptist churches of Western Pennsylvania, Virginia, and Ohio, over a wide region.

An opportunity unexpectedly presented itself, in a section of the country where his fame as an able and logical speaker had preceded him, which was destined to furnish him with one of the most effective means for the advancement of his views. This was an invitation to engage in public debate in defense of the Baptist cause. It is a mistake, however, at this or any other period of his life, to regard him as a professional controversialist, never happy except when engaged in measuring lances with some theological antagonist, or assailing the religious views of others. Such a conception does great injustice to his generous nature. To put an end to religious controversy had, from the beginning, been one of the chief aims of the movement which he advocated. His father had declared at the formation of the "Christian Association," that "though written objections to the proposed movement would be thankfully received and seriously considered, verbal controversy was absolutely refused." When the mantle of leadership fell upon the shoulders of Alexander Campbell, he strove to adhere to the same policy, shrank from public discussion, and was only drawn into it when any other course would have been attributed to the weakness of his cause. He was never the aggressor, though at a later period he became favorably disposed to this means of disseminating his views; but when the challenge came, he was the last man to shrink from a manly and honorable defense of what he held to be the truth.

Thus he was drawn into five celebrated public discussions of questions covering a wide field of investigation, from the scriptural mode and meaning of Christian baptism to the defense of Protestantism against the Papacy, and of Christianity against infidelity. In every instance he proved himself an able defender of the truth as he found it in the Christian Scriptures.

The first call to engage in public, oral discussion came to Mr. Campbell in the spring of 1820. The jealousy of rival religious parties in an Ohio village led to a controversy between two preachers, one a Seceder, the other a Baptist. The dispute ended in a challenge by Rev. John Walker, the Seceder minister, to meet any Baptist minister of good standing, in the public discussion of the question of baptism. The high opinion entertained throughout that region of Mr. Campbell's ability, led to his selection as the most suitable champion of such a cause. At first he declined to engage in the discussion, "not regarding public debate as the proper method of proceeding in contending for the faith once delivered to the saints." Repeated and urgent solicitation was made by his friends. Conscious of his own powers, possessed of dauntless courage, and fearing that his refusal might be interpreted as a confession of the weakness of the Baptist ground, he at last yielded to the pressure and accepted the challenge.

All preliminaries being arranged, the discussion was begun on June 19, at Mt. Pleasant, Ohio. The chief point of controversy was the scriptural authority for infant baptism; but before the close of the debate it took a wider range, including the whole baptismal controversy as it was at that time waged between Baptist and Pedo-baptist. As the discussion proceeded, all recognized that the Baptist cause had found an invincible defender. His whole training had fitted him for such an arena. His liberal education, his vast reading, his remarkable memory, his rare powers of generalization, his splendid diction, his admirable self-control, sustained as they were by deep earnestness of purpose, gave him at once a vantage ground which he never relinquished. But such was the originality of his method in handling truth, and his freedom from the accepted nomenclature of the schools, that even the victory, which was universally admitted to be with him, was not accepted by his Baptist brethren as an unmixed blessing. The effect of this discussion, however, was to add to Mr. Campbell's growing reputation. His fame was widely extended by the publication of the debate, which was read by thousands, and began soon to produce results far beyond the fondest hopes of the young reformer.

Meanwhile affairs in the Redstone Association were not improving. The success of his debate with Walker, while enlarging his circle of admirers, at the same time multiplied his antagonists. The leaders of the opposition in the Association continued their charges of heresy, and were ready to resort to any means that would increase the prejudice against him, and secure his excommunication. At last, wearied by the continued hostility of his enemies, Mr. Campbell determined to place himself beyond the bounds of their jurisdiction. He had received a cordial invitation to become a member of the Mahoning Association, which embraced the Baptist churches of Eastern Ohio, and as he had already been cordially received by the preachers and churches of that region, he determined to accept. In order to make the change with as little friction as possible, he took a letter from the Brush Run Church, and with thirty others organized a new church at Wellsburg, Va., which applied for membership, and was at once received in the Mahoning Association. Thus, in the month of August, 1823, was organized the second church of the Reformation, and by this means Alexander Campbell escaped excommunication from the Baptist Church, which would certainly have been his fate had he longer remained a member of the Redstone Association.

Chapter Seven:
"THE CHRISTIAN BAPTIST"

In his early contributions to the secular newspapers, already mentioned, Alexander Campbell displayed a talent that was destined to become a most efficient agency in the dissemination of truth. He could write in a clear, persuasive style that carried conviction. It was several years, however, before he thought of using the printed page in the extension of the cause he had espoused. His appreciation of the power of the press seems to have dated from his debate with Walker. Such was the interest manifested in that discussion, that it was published in a volume of some four hundred pages, was widely read, running through several editions, and was instrumental in awakening an earnest spirit of inquiry among the thoughtful people of all creeds.

The success attending this published debate, and the numerous inquiries it brought him concerning his views, led Mr. Campbell, for the first time, to cherish a hope that something might be done on a more extended scale to restore religious society to its primitive simplicity. He now began to realize the greatness of his religious discoveries, and felt himself called to a wider field. Traveling up and down the country on his trusted horse, he preached wherever he could get men to listen, a crusade against religious corruptions, with all the fire and zeal of a Peter the Hermit. These early excursions took him through portions of Pennsylvania, Virginia, and Ohio; and wherever he went his plea was for the new order of things, or rather a return to the faith, customs, and practices of the apostolic church.

The demands of so wide a field called for new methods in its cultivation; so he resolved to call to his assistance the printing press. He now conceived of a work in monthly parts, to be devoted to the interests of the reformation. The design was warmly approved by his friends. Only as regards the title of the work was there difference of opinion. Mr. Campbell, and those who shared his convictions at that time, occupied a peculiar position. Though identified with the Baptist Church, they were earnestly pleading for a broader, undenominational fellowship.

As a matter of expediency the title *Christian Baptist* was agreed upon, and, in the spring of 1823, a prospectus was issued announcing the new monthly, the first number of which appeared on July 4, of that year. Its appearance marks an era in religious history. Its like had never been seen in current religious literature.

> *The Christian Baptist,* said its editor, *shall espouse the cause of no religious sect, excepting that ancient sect "called Christians first at Antioch." Its sole object shall be the eviction of truth, and the exposing of error in doctrine and practice. The editor, acknowledging no standard of religious faith or works other than the Old and New Testament, and the latter as the only standard of the religion of Jesus Christ, will, intentionally at least, oppose nothing which it contains and recommend nothing which it does not enjoin. Having no worldly interest at stake from the adoption or reprobation of any articles of faith or religious practice, having no gift nor religious emolument to blind his eyes or to pervert his judgment, he hopes to manifest that he is an impartial advocate of truth.*[1]

A glance at the subjects treated in the early numbers of the *Christian Baptist* reveals its independent, aggressive spirit. There are essays written in the editor's trenchant style on "The Christian Religion," giving in comprehensive outline the sublime purpose and plan of human redemption; on "The Clergy," rebuking in strong terms their "unwarranted presumption, bigotry, sectarianism, and venality;" on "Ecclesiastical Characters, Councils, Creeds and Sects," unfolding the history of the apostasy of the church, and the origin of its weakening divisions; on "The Restoration of the Ancient Order of Things," portraying the customs and practices of the Church of the New Testament; and on "Christian Union," pointing to the New Testament basis as the only practical ground of unity.

It was a veritable John the Baptist in religious journalism.

---

[1] *Memoirs of Alexander Campbell*, Vol. 2, page 50.

Its continuous message was a call to repentance to erring ecclesiasts. It at once fearlessly attacked whatever it conceived to
be a corruption of, or departure from, the New Testament
standard; and it fell like a fire-brand into hundreds of widely
scattered communities, and everywhere provoked a spirit of
inquiry.

To the new duties of editor, without abating in the least his
labors along other lines, Mr. Campbell now devoted himself
with characteristic energy. That he might take entire supervi-
sion of the work, he set up a printing establishment on his farm
on the Buffalo. Purchasing the necessary supplies, erecting a
suitable building, and engaging the help of practical printers, he
became, at once, proprietor, business manager, editor, leading
contributor, proofreader, mailing clerk, all in one. This involved no small amount of labor, for in the first seven years the
little country printing-office issued of his own works more than
forty thousand volumes. To get an adequate idea of his great
industry at this period, it must be remembered, that, in addition
to the labors incident upon his publishing enterprise, he continued regularly to preach, attended to an extensive correspondence, and gave personal attention to the improvement and
cultivation of a large farm.

It was in connection with the publication of the *Christian
Baptist* that the name Bethany was attached to the spot hallowed by the memory of this great man. The earlier issues of
the magazine were carried to the neighboring village of West
Liberty, four miles distant, for mailing. As its circulation increased, this was found to be inconvenient, and, at the solicitation of Mr. Campbell, a post-office was established in his own
residence, to which he gave the name Bethany. He was himself
appointed the first postmaster, and continued to hold the office
for thirty years, through successive administrations and political changes.

During the preparation of the early numbers of the *Christian Baptist*, Mr. Campbell was arranging the preliminaries for
another public discussion. Mr. McCalla, a Presbyterian
preacher of Kentucky, in the spring of 1823, intimated his
willingness to engage Mr. Campbell in a discussion of the

question of baptism, that he might retrieve the injury which had been done his cause by Mr. Walker's admitted failure. Mr. Campbell, having ascertained his standing, agreed to meet him, and arrangement was made for the discussion to take place in October, in the town of Washington, Ky. The low stage of the Ohio River necessitated Mr. Campbell's making the entire journey on horseback.

Here, as in his former discussion, the entire bearing of the baptismal question was carefully canvassed. It is not necessary, at this point, to go into the details of the arguments pro and con. Each controverted point was hotly contested in the presence of a vast assemblage, which had been drawn together by Mr. Campbell's reputation and their interest in the question at issue. During this discussion, which lasted seven days, in addition to his defense of the scriptural mode and subject of baptism, Mr. Campbell gradually, for the first time, unfolded its design and true place in the economy of the Gospel, though it was several years before any use was made of it in urging obedience to Christ.

While the Baptist ministers, who were in attendance at the debate, recognized him as their strongest champion and were enthusiastic over his defense of their favorite tenet, he did not desire to enjoy a larger share of their good will than he deserved. Consequently, during the progress of the discussion, he met a company of them and stated the grounds he held which might not be acceptable to them. From the first three numbers of the *Christian Baptist*, which he carried with him, he read extracts from his essays, boldly setting forth his reformatory views. So favorably were they received at that time, that he was invited to extend his tour among the Baptist churches of Kentucky.

The untiring effort of Mr. Campbell during these years, as we have seen, was for the liberation of Christian society from the thralldom of human tradition and priestly domination. He had long since come to believe that the only hope of uniting Christendom was through a return to the primitive order, as found in the New Testament. He saw only one way to the accomplishment of such a result, that was to put men really and fully into the possession of the Bible. Martin Luther had unchained the Scriptures and given them to the people in their own tongues. Chillingworth had declared that "the Bible and the Bible alone is the religion of Protestants." But it was Mr. Campbell's mission to put the people into actual possession of the Bible, by convincing them that it could be understood, and inducing them to study it.

Through the pages of the *Christian Baptist* he sought continually to bring the Bible before the people. Instead of creeds, he held aloft the Word of God, and urged men to read it for themselves. He believed that if it was given as a revelation from God to man, the people ought to be able to understand it. He taught that by employing the same common-sense methods in its study that were used in dealing with other books, it would beam with intelligent meaning. Some hints of his are so essential to a knowledge of the revealed truth of the Gospel that I transcribe them from the pages of the *Christian Baptist*:

> *Begin with Matthew's Gospel; read the whole of it at one reading or two; mark on the margin every sentence you think you do not understand. Turn back again, read it a second time in less portions at once than in the first reading; cancel such marks as you have made which noted passages which on the first reading appeared to you dark or difficult to understand, but on the second reading opened to your view. Then read Mark, Luke, and John in the same manner. After having read each evangelist in this way, read them all in succession a third time. At this time you will be able, no doubt, to cancel many of your marks. Then read the Acts of the Apostles, which is the key to all the Epistles; then the Epistles in a similar manner. Always before reading an Epistle, read everything said about the people addressed in the Epistle, which you find in the Acts of the Apostles… In pursuing this plan, we have no doubt, in getting even three times through the New Testament, that you will learn much more of the Christian religion than a learned divine*

could teach you in seven years.[1]

In a course so radical and so at variance with accepted notions as that now advocated by Mr. Campbell through the columns of the *Christian Baptist*, it was but natural that he should awaken the bitter opposition of the ministry. The fire of his enemies resounded from every quarter. In response to their attacks, he thundered the authority of the Word of God. The severity of his strictures upon the clergy at that period may seem a little harsh to our ears. But we must remember that religious conditions differed widely from those with which we are familiar, and that when he spoke in condemnation of the clergy, he meant that class who "assumed to be the solely authorized expositors of the sacred oracles, denying to the people the right or the power of comprehending or interpreting the Scripture for themselves." It was against these false assumptions, which he felt to be the most serious barriers to Gospel triumph, that he uttered his most withering denunciations.

"We are convinced," he wrote, "fully convinced that the whole head is sick and the whole heart faint, of modern fashionable Christianity." Feeling that the "clerical machinery," as he called it, was responsible for the unfortunate condition of religious society, Mr. Campbell could scarcely find terms strong enough to express his disapproval of the methods by which the whole system was maintained. Hence it was that he attacked, as unworthy of the religion of the lowly Nazarene, "costly meeting-houses and organs, selling pews, missionary wheels and boxes," and various other features employed as adjuncts to sectarian growth.

In his opposition to sectarianism, nothing that contributed to its success escaped his denunciation. He was even for a time led to condemn Sunday-schools, missionary, educational, and Bible societies, because as then conducted, he thought they fostered the denominational spirit. So radical were his views at this time that his own friends became alarmed. They feared that he would defeat the noble enterprise in which he was engaged

---

[1] *Memoirs of Alexander Campbell*, Vol. 2, page 96.

by "overstepping the fixed boundaries of truth;" that in has-
tening out of Babylon, he was about to run past Jerusalem. They
frankly told him of his error, and urged a milder and more
conciliatory course, a suggestion which at a later period he
seemed disposed to adopt.

The effect of the *Christian Baptist* was almost magical. It,
of course, met with the most bitter denunciation from those
whose authority it attacked. Pastors forbade their flocks reading
it, and it was treated as an incarnation of evil. But it found a
wide reading and ready acceptance among another class. Many
there were, who, wearied with the denominational strife, and
restive under ecclesiastical denomination, awaited a prophet
whose aim was spiritual emancipation, and whose strong and
fearless leadership they could trust. To such the *Christian
Baptist* was a welcome visitor. Copies accidentally falling into
the hands of earnest inquirers led to conviction. Thus as early as
1824, James Challen, a talented young student, was led to es-
pouse the cause advocated by the *Christian Baptist*; and about
the same time P.S. Fall and D.S. Burnett, both gifted defenders
of the faith, joined the ranks of the reformers. That first generation of pioneer preachers, whose names were household words
with our fathers, were largely led to join with Mr. Campbell in
his efforts to restore the primitive church through the pages of
the *Christian Baptist*. No single agency employed in the advocacy of the movement was ever productive of wider or more
lasting results. So great was the demand for it at a later period,
that it was republished in an abridged form, and has since run
through several editions. Today no stronger or better statement
of the fundamental principles advocated by the Christian
Church can be found than in the pages of the *Christian Baptist*.

Mr. Campbell's success as an editor was far beyond his
expectations. While as late as 1825, only three churches, those
at Brush Run, Pittsburg, and Wellsburg, had accepted his restoration ideas, the leaven had been planted over a wide section,
and had already begun to work. A spirit of inquiry was being
awakened, and many, like those of Berea, were "searching the
Scriptures daily, whether those things were so."

Chapter Eight:
RELIGIOUS DISSENSIONS

It had never been the purpose of Alexander Campbell to become the founder of another religious society, and this denial he now repeated with emphasis. "I have no idea of adding to the catalogue of new sects," he wrote in the *Christian Baptist* of 1826. "I labor to see sectarianism abolished and all Christians of every name united upon the one foundation upon which the apostolic church was founded. To bring Baptists and Pedo-baptists to this is my supreme end."

In this great movement toward unity, he had hoped to see the Baptists take the initiative. Notwithstanding his experiences with the Redstone Association, he had come to hold them in high esteem, and to regard them as nearer the primitive pattern than any other religious denomination. "I hope," he wrote, "I will not be accused of sectarian partiality, when I avow my conviction that the Baptist society have as much liberality in their views, as much of the ancient simplicity of the Christian Church, as much of the spirit of Christianity about them, as are to be found among any other people." In his assault upon the "clergy" he was careful to distinguish between those whom he included in his denunciation and the "ministers of the Baptist and other independent churches." These, with few exceptions, he had found to be conscientious and fair-minded men.

But he did not let his admiration for this people blind his eyes to their imperfections. He was frank to declare: "That there is in the views and practices of this large and widely-extended community a great need of reformation and of a restoration of the ancient order of things, few will contradict." That he might lead them into clearer views of the Gospel now consumed all his energies. With this aim he felt justified in continuing his connection with the Baptist Church, and through it achieving his fond desire of the union of Christ's followers on a broad, scriptural basis. "I do intend," he said, "to continue in connection with this people, so long as they will permit me to say what I believe, to teach what I am assured of, and to censure what is amiss in their views and practices."

At this period Mr. Campbell was very much encouraged with the progress of reform sentiments. In his extended tours among the Baptist churches of Ohio and Kentucky, he was everywhere well received. Large and enthusiastic audiences listened daily to his plea, and often to a late hour at night he was beset by "crowds of anxious inquirers, who sought religious information and counsel." Here and there churches avowed their determination henceforth to be guided by the Bible alone, and many of the leading preachers of the denomination were earnestly searching the Scriptures "whether these things were so." As an example of the curious regard in which Mr. Campbell was then held, we quote from John Smith, afterward a most successful advocate of the reformation in Kentucky. Upon his first meeting with Mr. Campbell, he said:

> I then felt as if I wanted to sit down and look at him for one hour, without hearing a word from any one. I wanted to scan him who had been so much talked of, and who had, in the "Christian Baptist" and in his debates, introduced so many new thoughts into my mind.

Cheered by his hearty reception by the Baptist churches, and by the progress of liberal views among them, Mr. Campbell was encouraged to write:

> In one thing they may appear, in time to come, proudly singular and pre-eminently distinguished. Mark it well. Their historian, in the year 1900, may say, "We are the only people who would tolerate, or ever did tolerate, any person to continue as a reformer or restorer among us. While other sects excluded all who would have enlarged their views and exalted their virtues, while every Jerusalem in Christendom stoned its own prophets, and exiled its own best friends, and compelled them to set up for themselves, we constitute the only exception of this kind in the annals of Christianity,—nay in the annals

of the world." [1]

That he might hasten the progress of reform and awaken a new interest in the study of the Scripture, Mr. Campbell undertook the work, in the winter of 1826, of preparing and publishing a new version of the New Testament. To this task every spare moment was devoted. While the work was largely a compilation from George Campbell's new version of the Gospels, Doddridge's translation of the Acts of the Apostles and Revelation, and MacKnight's free rendering of the Epistles, he made a careful revision of the whole, comparing the various renderings and selecting the one which seemed more clear and accurate. To these, besides a valuable introduction to New Testament study, he contributed such hints and aids as might be conducive to a correct understanding of the sacred writings, and published them in a volume of five hundred pages, entitled "The Living Oracles." His purpose was to foster a spirit of inquiry, as well as to aid in an understanding of the message of Revelation.

As was to be expected, this version was received with disfavor by Pedo-baptists generally, because in translating, instead of Anglicizing, the word for baptism, he left no ground or excuse for the prevailing practice. But it is doubtful if any version of the New Testament ever contained a clearer or more faithful revelation of the teachings of Christ and his apostles.

A series of events now transpired which changed the religious situation, blasted Mr. Campbell's hopes of a continued reformation within the borders of the Baptist Church, and set him adrift with a large following, but without denominational ties.

The first storm-center was the old Redstone Association. Its ruling spirits had never ceased to cherish a feeling of hostility toward Mr. Campbell. The appearance of the *Christian Baptist* had intensified this feeling. Some of its representatives now traveled up and down the country, publicly attacking him and grossly misrepresenting his teachings. He was charged with

---

[1] *Memoirs of Alexander Campbell*, Vol. 2, page 135.

denying the necessity of the new birth and with rejecting heart-religion. He was denounced as a breeder of heresy and sedition, and undeserving of fellowship or recognition among Baptist churches.

At the annual meeting of the Association in 1827, the crisis came. Mr. Campbell had been appointed corresponding messenger from the Mahoning to the Redstone Association that year.

As his letter of greeting made no reference to the Philadelphia Confession, the accepted standard of the Baptist Church, it was determined by his enemies that he should not be received. Upon a canvass it was found that they could rally to their support but ten of the twenty-three churches of the Association; but with these ten they ventured the hazardous experiment of excluding the other thirteen, and organized themselves upon the basis of their cherished creed. The thirteen churches denied admission then formed a new association, declaring as the second article of their constitution, "We receive the Scriptures as the only rule of faith and practice to all the churches of Christ." Thus began the conflict which within the next three years resulted in the complete separation of Baptists and those who accepted the principles of the reformation.

In the same year a meeting was held by the Mahoning Association which was destined to lead to important consequences. At that meeting a young man, Walter Scott by name, an ardent admirer of Alexander Campbell, who had entered heartily into all his plans, was appointed to do itinerant preaching among the churches of the Western Reserve, Ohio. The Baptist churches at that time, with few exceptions, were in a languishing condition. Conversions were few, and indifference widespread. The seventeen churches which comprised the Association reported only sixteen converts to Christ for the year 1825. But the entrance of Walter Scott into the evangelistic field marked a new era for the churches of this section. A tidal wave of revival was at once set in motion, which continued to attend Mr. Scott's ministry wherever he went, and by the close of his first year he was able to report a thousand converts.

The preaching of this young man marks a new era in modern evangelism. He had studied the Word of God long and prayerfully. Its message and method had smitten his heart, and he resolved, at the beginning of his evangelistic labors, to try the experiment of preaching the Gospel according to the New Testament model, urging men to accept Christ upon the terms offered by Peter on the day of Pentecost. As might be expected, a message so antagonistic to the prevailing instruction of the times, would soon encounter opposition and misrepresentation. Preachers warned their congregations against him. He was charged with preaching water salvation, and ignoring essential spiritual changes. In spite of this opposition, he was well received by the Baptist churches forming the Association for which he labored. Wherever he went among them they speedily fell into his way of thinking, and most of them abandoned their creeds and customs for the simple practice of the New Testament, though still affiliating with the Baptist Church.

The success of Walter Scott in the Western Reserve secured him an invitation to the Baptist Church at Sharon, Pa., which proved the second storm-center of the religious dissensions that threatened the peace of Baptist society. The labors of Mr. Scott at this place were attended with his usual success. On a simple profession of their faith in Jesus as the Son of God, they were baptized in the river nearby. But no sooner had the evangelist left, than the conservative portion of the church determined to reject the new converts as having failed to conform to Baptist usages, and to exclude from their fellowship all who shared in Mr. Scott's way of thinking. These members, deprived of religious fellowship, formed a new organization on broad, New Testament principles and independent of the jurisdiction of any religious association.

The feeling against Mr. Campbell's friends and sympathizers now became so intense in many sections that those of the old Baptist faith and order refused longer to fellowship them. In the spring of 1830, the Third Baptist Church of Philadelphia excluded all Mr. Campbell's followers, who at once organized themselves into an independent congregation. The work thus begun spread rapidly. Documents denouncing Mr. Campbell's writings and branding him as a heretic, were diligently circulated by partisan bigotry, and every means used to destroy his influence with the churches. As a result, Baptists were led almost everywhere to separate themselves from the reformers. Unable to check the spirit of discord and intolerance that now swept the church, Mr. Campbell calmly awaited the results, at the same time disavowing any responsibility for the dissensions which he lamented. In reply to the attacks of his enemies, he wrote:

> *If there be a division, gentlemen, you will make it, not I; and the more you oppose us with the weight of your censure, like the palm tree, we will grow the faster. I am for peace, for union, for harmony, for cooperation with all good men. But I fear you not; if you fling firebrands, arrows, and discords into the army of the faith, you will repent it, not we. You will lose influence, not we. We covet not persecution, but we disregard it. We fear nothing but error, and should you proceed to make divisions, you will find that they will reach much farther than you are aware, and that the time is past when an anathema from an association will produce any other effect than contempt from some and a smile from others.* [1]

The result was as Mr. Campbell had predicted. The principles of the reformation were much more widely spread than his defamers had expected. In some instances churches were rent asunder; in others entire churches were excluded from fellowship with Baptist Associations; and in others entire Associations ceased to call themselves Baptist. This was notably true of the churches of the Western Reserve. When the Mahoning Association met in the autumn of 1830, such had been the leavening influence of Walter Scott's evangelism that it unanimously resolved that it should never meet again as "an advisory council;" and so, ceased connection with the Baptist Church, which had already, as a denomination, repudiated all who were tinctured with the principles advocated by Alexander

---

[1] *Memoirs of Alexander Campbell*, Vol. 2, page 323.

Campbell and his co-laborers. From this point dates the separate existence of the religious body known as the Disciples of Christ, of whose aims and views we shall have something to say in another chapter.

In the midst of the religious strife which led to the separation of Baptists and Disciples, a great sorrow flung its shadow across Mr. Campbell's pathway. He had always been attached to his home by the strongest ties. Though called away from its enjoyment much of the time by the growing demands of the cause in which he labored, it was to its hallowed precinct that he returned to find a haven from the storms that raged about him. But in 1827, while calumny and misrepresentation were ringing on every side, his ears were made deaf to all in the sorrow that came into his heart in the loss of his companion. After sixteen years of happiness his home was left desolate. Forbidden to sorrow as those who have no hope, he accepted his loss with Christian resignation, but his sadness found expression in the subdued spirit which for the time characterized all his utterances; and it continued to be a beautiful custom of his to commemorate his first marriage on each recurring anniversary.

A figure so commanding as Mr. Campbell had now become could not fail to attract attention outside of religious circles. In his case public recognition was not wanting. Though often solicited, only once did he venture on the stormy sea of politics. That was in 1829. Steps were being taken toward the revision of the Constitution of the State in which he lived. He was urged by his friends to become a candidate for a seat in the Virginia Constitutional Convention. The people of West Virginia felt that undue power was given to, and exerted by, the slaveholders of the eastern part of the State. It was desirable that the constitution be so amended as to guarantee equal rights to the non-slaveholders of the western portion. Mr. Campbell was recognized, by those acquainted with him, as one capable of faithfully and powerfully representing their interests, and at last consented to become their candidate, only on condition that he would not be required to take the stump.

Once in the field, it was discovered that a combination was

being formed to secure his defeat. In the emergency he consented to deliver a number of addresses. In this new role he showed a capacity which, had he chosen to devote himself to politics, would have secured him almost any office in the gift of the people.

> *His large and varied knowledge, his love of all mankind, his inimitable powers of conversation, even sporting and playing in the most easy and graceful way with subjects from the most abstruse to the simplest,—these would have endeared him to the great commonalty, and perpetually have secured him their enthusiastic support. Thus his elevation to the highest place in the gift of the people would have been certain. And once high in power, the masterly manner in which he would have handled the great questions of state, would have made him the idol of his own people and the admiration of all civilized nations.[1]*

As the result of a spirited canvass he was elected; and as a member of a distinguished body which numbered among its representatives James Madison and James Monroe, former Presidents of the United States, he rendered valuable service. In the face of the growing arrogance of the slave power, he was unable to secure for his constituents the recognition they demanded; but his able presentation of their cause secured him wide recognition and esteem at a time when his religious enemies were seeking by means of vituperation and slander to secure his downfall.

True to his position as a minister, he did not allow political interests to obscure his religious position. He rather endeavored to make his position as a member of the convention contribute to the furtherance of the cause of the kingdom, which was dearer to him than any earthly interest. In private conversation with distinguished persons of the convention, and in public addresses on every Lord's day during his stay in Richmond, he urged the one great theme of the primitive Gospel, thus con-

---

[1] *Lard's Quarterly*, Vol. 3, page 257.

tributing, in large measure, to the success which soon attended the movement throughout the State.

Chapter Nine:
THE CHRISTIAN CHURCH

We have now traced the career of Alexander Campbell to a point where the largest success awaited his effort. In 1830, when the doors of Baptist fellowship closed behind him and those who shared his convictions, he was in the zenith of his great powers. Whether held in esteem or regarded with hatred, he was everywhere looked upon as an extraordinary man, and wherever he went multitudes thronged to hear.

While yet in the prime of life, Mr. Campbell was permitted to witness the fruit of his own planting in the triumph of a great principle. Twenty years of tireless effort had resulted in widespread interest in the cause for which he pleaded. Religious communions, reproducing the essential characteristics of the primitive church as revealed in the New Testament, sprang up into independent congregations, wherever his plea for the restoration of primitive Christianity had been carried. Calls now came to him from all parts of the country for instruction and guidance in the principles which he advocated. Men often came hundreds of miles to see him, always returning convinced of the correctness of his views. These calls were often answered by long tours, which, in the absence of railroads, were attended by many hardships, but contributed largely to the success of the movement. The extent of his labors as the apostle of undenominational Christianity may be gathered from a brief extract from one of his letters:

> *It has been with me a sermon of three months' continuance, interrupted only by the stages of a journey of some three thousand miles. My public addresses have been in Virginia thirty-four, in South Carolina twenty-three, in Georgia twenty, in South Alabama ten, besides some hundred fireside sermons almost as laborious as those in public assemblies.*

Like his venerable father, Mr. Campbell had shrunk from the responsibility of any further division of religious society.

But now that it had been effected by the exclusion of his followers from their old church relationship, his great labor was to secure their reorganization after the Divine Model, which he ever kept before him. This was no small task. Heterogeneous elements, representing the various schools of religious thought and the various forms of church polity, were brought together in many communities, drawn by an intense desire to effect the unity of the church by a return to apostolic precedent and practice. But as men came out of their respective folds to unite on the one foundation, they were confronted by many difficult problems. There were questions of expediency, matters of opinion, forms of administration, to settle. Should they adopt the methods of their religious neighbors or be totally unlike them? Should they have Sunday-schools and organized missionary effort, and other forms of religious cooperation? Or should they class these along with innovations of doctrine and practice against which the whole movement was a protest?

To the solution of these questions, Mr. Campbell now applied himself, and, as heretofore, appealed, wherever appeal was possible, to the only infallible guide known to him, the teachings of the divinely-inspired apostles. His conception of the church as a divinely-authorized association of believers is thus stated:

> It is a society of disciples professing to believe the one grand fact, the Messiahship of Jesus, voluntarily submitting to his authority and guidance, having all of them in their baptism expressed their faith in him and their allegiance to him, and statedly meeting together in one place to walk in all his commandments and ordinances. This society, with its bishop or bishops and its deacon may require, is perfectly independent of any tribunal on earth called ecclesiastical.[1]

Henceforth his mission was to watch and foster the development of such a society, not as an authoritative leader, but as a friendly patron and adviser.

---

[1] *Memoirs of Alexander Campbell*, Vol. 2, page 58.

The separation of Baptists and Disciples led Mr. Campbell to discontinue the *Christian Baptist,* which, as the organ of the reformatory movement, had since 1823 accomplished so much, in the spread of its principles. He now feared that the name of the paper would be given to the advocates of the reformation. Against all divisive and party designations he had contended from the beginning, and he desired to remove all possibility of such result. In the final number of the *Christian Baptist,* issued July 5, 1830, he thus states his reason for its discontinuance:

> *I have commenced a new work and taken a new name for it on various accounts. Hating sects and sectarian names, I resolved to prevent the name of Christian Baptist from being fixed upon us, to do which efforts were making. It is true men's tongues are their own, and they may use them as they please, but I am re-solved to give them no just occasion for nicknaming advocates for the ancient order of things.[1]*

But in seeking to secure his followers against the name Christian Baptists, Mr. Campbell was called to defend them against a party designation in every way more obnoxious to him. Recognizing him as the leader of the movement which was everywhere rapidly winning favor with the people, his religious enemies sought to bring reproach upon the cause which he advocated by branding it as *Campbellism* and his followers as *Campbellites.* He modestly disclaimed the honor of being the founder of a religious denomination, and resented, with all the earnestness of his nature, the attempt to fasten his name upon the growing brotherhood which shared his convictions. His answer to those guilty of this uncharitable designation was:

> *It is a nickname of reproach invented and adopted by those whose views, feelings, and desires are all sec-tarian; who cannot conceive of Christianity in any other light than an **ism**. These isms are now the real reproach of those who adopt them, as they are the*

---

[1] *Christian Baptist*, page 665.

intended reproaches of those who originate and apply them. He that gives them when they are disclaimed violates the express law of Christ. He speaks evil against his brother, and is accounted a railer and reviler, and placed along with the haters of God and those who have no lot in the kingdom of heaven. They who adopt them out of choice, disown the Christ and insult him; for they give the honor, which is due to him alone, to the creature of the devil, for all slander and detraction are of the creation of the devil. If Christians were wholly cast into the mold of the apostles' doctrine, they would feel themselves as much aggrieved and slandered in being called by any man's name as they would in being called a thief, a fornicator, or a drunkard.[1]

Mr. Campbell always contended that scriptural things should be spoken of in scriptural terms. It was his conviction that denominational titles were more than half the cause of the continuance of party spirit. To the Scriptures, therefore, he went for a name for God's children. It was his desire that this name, in addition to being scriptural, should be comprehensive enough to include all who love the Lord. He found in that ancient church, which he had taken as his model, various names applied expressive of different relationships, but any of them broad enough to include the whole brotherhood of Christ. Because of their faith they were called Believers; because of their consecration and purity, Saints; in their relation to each other, Brethren; in their relation to the Great Teacher, Disciples; at Antioch, where the first Gentile church was established, Christians. Mr. Campbell preferred the name *Disciples* of Christ as the more humble appellation. Walter Scott, who shared in all his counsels, urged the name *Christian* as the more comprehensive, and better than any or all others describing the relation of the saint to the Savior. Mr. Campbell feared that the adoption of the name Christian, which had already been ap-

---

[1] *Christian Baptist*, page 451.

propriated by a people regarded as denying the divinity of Christ, would make his brethren an object of undeserved reproach and misrepresentation among the so-called orthodox churches. It was unfortunate that these good men could not have come to an agreement, and saved the interminable confusion that has since resulted from the interchangeable or local use of the name "Disciples of Christ," "Christians," "Churches of Christ," etc.

These churches, meanwhile, by whatever designation known, were multiplying with phenomenal rapidity. The proscriptive measures employed against them by the bitter partisan spirit of the times, proved an aid rather than a hindrance to the general diffusion of their principles among all parties, and led many from the various denominations to adopt the faith and doctrine of the primitive church. While not a few of the accessions to the newly-organized churches came from the ranks of other religious communions, the movement was attended by an almost "unprecedented success in the conversion of those who had not, as yet, embraced any of the religious systems of the day." These churches presented to modern religious society many distinctive features which had been obscured by the accumulated theological rubbish of the centuries. Mr. Campbell had said, "I believe if we would brush aside the creeds and traditions, we would find a simple and sufficient rule of faith in the New Testament." Acting on this suggestion, Christian communions sprang up which, without a written creed, other than that inscribed by the pen of inspiration, have presented and preserved a marvelous unity in the essential elements of Christian faith.

A brief survey of the principles for which these churches contended in 1830 is here in place. In their plea for the restoration of primitive Christianity, neither Mr. Campbell nor those who joined him in his search for a scriptural ideal, rejected everything that their religious neighbors held. In many vital and essential respects they were happy to find themselves in perfect agreement with other evangelical churches, not on the authority of their creeds and confessions, but on the authority of the Word of God. These points of agreement were more numerous, in fact, than the points of difference, and embraced belief in the inspiration of the Holy Scriptures and their all-sufficiency, the divine excellency of Jesus as the Son of God, the personal and perpetual mission of the Holy Spirit, the sinfulness of the race and its need of regeneration, the necessity of faith, repentance, and a life of obedience, the perpetuity of baptism and the Lord's Supper, the obligation to fittingly observe the Lord's day, the recognition, of the church of Christ as a divine institution, the fullness and freeness of salvation, the final punishment of the ungodly, etc. But the course which they had thus far pursued in their search for the old paths led them to the discovery of other principles which have since constituted their distinctive peculiarities as a religious body.

1. The churches thus organized were unalterably pledged to the cause of Christian union. They believed and taught, on the authority of the Word, that divisions among the children of God were sinful, that denominationalism presented one of the greatest barriers to the triumph of truth, and that Christ's people must be united before any achievement commensurate with the greatness of his Gospel can be won. Every new church, therefore, became an added protest against existing division, and an added petition to Christ's prayer for the unity of the church.

2. They urged the acceptance of the New Testament as the only authoritative standard of Christian doctrine and the essential bond of Christian union. Creeds as authoritative statements of belief had, it was shown, always been divisive. If Christian union were to become an accomplished fact, it was absolutely necessary, they held, that the Bible should be made "to displace from their position all human creeds, confessions of faith and formularies of doctrine and church government, as being not only unnecessary, but really a means of perpetuating divisions." They felt assured that the New Testament presented a practical basis of union, and that when we are satisfied "to simply believe in, and implicitly obey Christ," our unseemly divisions will disappear, or, to use the language of Thomas Campbell, the accomplishment of practical unity in Christian fellowship awaited "the restoration of pure, primitive, apostolic Christianity, in letter and spirit; in principle and practice."

3. They recognized the simple confession of faith in Jesus as the Son of God and the world's Savior, as the only authorized statement of belief necessary to acceptance with God and membership in the church of Christ. The New Testament, which they accepted as their sole guide in all matters of religious duty, presented no other test of the correctness of a man's faith, than this simple statement of truth, sanctioned by Jesus and demanded by the apostles. Its one article, they contended, was "broad enough to take in every lover of Jesus, and narrow enough to exclude everyone who will not accept him as the divine Savior and Lord." This creed, given by Simon Peter in his confession of Christ and elsewhere in the New Testament, is stated in the words, "I believe that Jesus is the Christ, the Son of the living God." Upon this confession of faith, when accompanied by a heartfelt desire to follow and obey the Christ, candidates were admitted to baptism and church membership.

4. They adopted the customs and practices of the primitive church, as revealed in the inspired writings, not only because apostolic, but because presenting the only possible ground upon which the followers of Christ could unite. Having failed to find scriptural authority for the common practice of infant baptism, they had from the first abandoned it. Unable to find authority for effusion as baptism in the practice or precept of either Christ or his apostles, they became immersionists, a practice recognized by all evangelical Christians as valid baptism, and, therefore, presenting the only possible ground for the broader fellowship for which they contended. Finding in the apostolic age that the Lord's Table was spread in Christian assemblies on every first day of the week, they sought to adhere to the apostolic practice by a similar observance of this memorial feast. As respect to practical Christianity they enjoined "an entire conformity to the divine will, in heart as well as life," knowing that "nothing avails in Christ Jesus but a new creature," and that "without holiness no one shall see the Lord."

A better statement of the views and practices of the Disciples cannot be found than in Mr. Campbell's own language in defense of the Bible as a sufficient standard of faith.

We preach, said he, *in the words of that book the Gospel as promulgated by the apostles in Jerusalem. We use in all important matters the exact words of inspiration. We command all men to believe, repent, and bring forth fruits worthy of reformation. We enjoin the same good works commanded by the Lord and by his apostles. We receive men of all denominations under heaven, of all sects and parties, who will make the good confession on which Jesus Christ builded his church. We propound that confession of faith in the identical words of inspiration, so that they who avow it express a divine faith and build upon a consecrated foundation, a well-tried corner-stone. On a sincere confession of this faith we immerse all persons, and then present them with God's own book as their book of faith, piety, and morality. This is our most obnoxious offense against the partyism of this age.*[1]

One other characteristic of this newly-organized body of disciples, deserving our notice, is the progressive spirit which from the very beginning was cherished by the friends of the movement. The moment they cast aside creeds and turned to the Bible, unrestricted by the narrow boundaries of parties and sects, the great principles of the plan of redemption began to develop in succession. It would say little for the depth and perfection of the Bible, if, even with the acknowledged learning and talent of such a leader as Mr. Campbell, the whole system had been comprehended at once. Many surprising discoveries had been made since the little church at Brush Run had been organized on the Bible alone. The truth that first struck their attention was the unity of the church. Next, consistency with their own principles led them into the waters of baptism; then, ten years later, to discover from the Word the definite object of immersion, and later still they learned to proclaim the Gospel to sinners in terms which Peter and Paul would have employed. That the church of 1830 had fathomed the depth or compre-

---

[1] *Campbell and Rice Debate*, page 783.

hended the fullness of divine wisdom, none for a moment claimed, but they rejoiced in their freedom from creed-barriers, which in other religious communions had put a check to further progress. Thanks to their liberal Christian policy, the church has since been able to make rapid progress in the discovery and application of religious truth.

The changed condition of the Disciples which followed their separation from the Baptists, demanded a change in the character of their instruction. The mission of the *Christian Baptist,* as we have seen, had been to awaken men to the evils of sectarianism, to lead them out of Egyptian bondage to ecclesiastical tradition. But now that the lines had been drawn, and he and his followers were denied fellowship with every existing religious organization, a new burden was laid upon Mr. Campbell and his co-laborers, that of gathering together their followers into organized communions and instructing them in the principles of the Gospel. The time had come when the keynote must be development, a going on to perfection. So he determined to start a new periodical, larger in size, different in character, and milder in tone.

The name of this new journal, *The Millennial Harbinger,* was expressive of Mr. Campbell's views regarding the coming millennial reign of Christ. The rapid spread of reformatory principles, his great success in combating infidelity and in correcting religious errors, led him to conceive of the millennial period as near at hand. This feeling was shared by Walter Scott and other of the pioneer preachers of the reformation. He did not at the time presume to fix upon any definite date, but as he advanced in years he became possessed of a conviction that the year 1866 would, in some way, usher in that period, and strangely enough, that was to him the year of the Lord's coming.

Through the columns of *The Millennial Harbinger,* Mr. Campbell was able to sway by the power of his pen, as he had done by his persuasive eloquence, the tide of religious conviction. Without abating a jot the importance of the principles advocated in his early editorial labors, he now unfolded those elements essential to higher development. Feeling that the success of the church would be measured by its missionary spirit, he in time became an advocate of missionary enterprises, and was chosen president of the American Christian Missionary Society, the first missionary organization among the Disciples.

Another problem that confronted Mr. Campbell, as new church organizations began to multiply, was the question of hymnology. The books then in use by other religious bodies contained sentiments not in accordance with the teachings of the New Testament. In his plea for pure speech, Mr. Campbell felt that the very hymns sung should breathe the spirit of New Testament Christianity. He therefore set about to compile a hymn-book from which unscriptural sentiments should be excluded, and in 1835 gave to the public a volume of two hundred pages filled with such selections as were true to Gospel facts and Gospel terms. This work was subsequently revised and enlarged, and before his death transferred to the American Christian Missionary Society, and is the basis of the Christian Hymnal still in use. To this collection he contributed several hymns himself which breathe his own lofty spirit of devotion.

Chapter Ten:
THE DEFENDER OF THE FAITH

The religious revival with which the century had opened, was checked while at its height, by the jealousies of contending religious parties. A state of religious apathy followed, which left the church powerless in the face of its foes. The prevailing indifference left the uncultivated soil to grow up in irreligion and unbelief. While churches wrangled over their creeds, the unconverted forsook the sanctuary; some to lament the departure of religious society from the revealed pattern which they found in their Bibles, and some to nurse their dissent into doubt, and doubt into unbelief.

Growing out of the unseemly strife engendered by denominational differences, society was threatened by another reign of skepticism. Infidel clubs were organized and flourished in almost every community. Infidel lecturers carried on their propaganda of unbelief with a zeal worthy of a noble cause. Everywhere, like Goliath, they breathed defiance against "the army of the living God," and challenged her leaders to come to the public defense of their creeds or acknowledge their ground irrational and untenable.

Heretofore Alexander Campbell had been occupied in delivering Christianity from its professed friends, but now that the work of restoration was fairly inaugurated, he marshaled all his resources to defend it from its open enemies. Few men were better fitted than he for such a task. Abandoning the outer defenses of theology, he established himself behind the impregnable fortress of revealed truth. He had no creed to defend but that ancient one which had withstood the onslaught of skepticism for eighteen hundred years. He acknowledged no authority but the Holy Scriptures and its incarnate Lord.

But his was the courage, not only of one who feels himself on safe ground, but of one who has thoroughly trained himself for the conflict. "Infidelity was one of those subjects which he had thoroughly investigated. His complete mastery of all possible trains of skeptical thought, and the comprehensiveness and penetrating power of his mind, unequaled in logical acumen, in ability to detect false arguments and discover true ones, and which could perceive in an instant the relations of proposition and proof, gave him an extraordinary power in such discussions which naturally sought every suitable opportunity to exert itself." He, accordingly, took peculiar pleasure in meeting the champions of unbelief, and never failed to win the admiration of believers of all creeds by his able defense of the common Faith.

The beginning of Mr. Campbell's defense of Christianity against the skepticism of the day was through the columns of the *Christian Baptist.* He at once made his magazine a forum, upon which men might freely present their difficulties and express their views, with a guarantee of fair and candid treatment from its editor. In this he won a favorable hearing from a large class who had not been able to accept the conclusions of current theology, or to choose between the creeds of contending parties, and was often able to remove the supposed obstacles to belief.

In 1828, Mr. Campbell was confronted by an antagonist worthy of his steel, in the person of Robert Owen, the acknowledged champion of infidelity, both in this country and Great Britain. Mr. Owen was a Scotch freethinker of wealth and scholarship. In 1824, he purchased a tract of land and established a community in Indiana, called New Harmony, for the application and development of his social views. A peculiar feature of this community was that all forms of religion should be rigidly excluded. Not content with building up an infidel community, he went forth as the apostle of free-thought, preaching a crusade against Christianity. During a series of lectures in New Orleans, early in 1828, Mr. Owen took occasion to challenge the clergy of that city to discuss with him the claims of the Christian religion.

> *I propose,* he said, *to prove, as I have already attempted to do in my lectures, that all the religions of the world have been founded on the ignorance of mankind; that they are directly opposed to the nev-*

er-changing laws of our nature; that they have been and are the real source of vice, disunion, and misery of every description; that they are now the only real bar to the formation of a society of virtue, of intelligence, of charity in its most extended sense, and of sincerity and kindness among the whole human family; and that they can no longer be maintained except through the ignorance of the mass of the people, and the tyranny of the few over that mass.[1]

As no response came from those addressed, Mr. Owen was about to embark for the Old World, boasting that no man in America dared to debate with him. But as soon as the news of this defiant attitude of the great champion of infidelity reached Mr. Campbell, he published the challenge in the *Christian Baptist,* and announced his readiness to accept it.

I have long wondered, he wrote, *why none of the public teachers of Christianity has appeared in defense of the last, best hope of mortal man. If none but Christian philosophers composed this society, it might be well enough to let Mr. Owen and his scheme of things find their own level. But while a few of the seniors disdain to notice, or affect to disdain, his scheme of things, it ought not to be forgotten that thousands are carried away as chaff before the wind by the apparently triumphant manner in which Mr. Owen moves along ... Relying on the Author, the reasonableness, and the excellency of the Christian religion, I will engage to meet Mr. Owen any time within one year from this date, at any place equidistant from New Harmony and Bethany, such as Cincinnati, Ohio, or Lexington, Ky., and will then and there undertake to show that Mr. Owen is utterly incompetent to prove the positions he has assumed, in a public debate.*[2]

---

[1] *Christian Baptist*, page 443.
[2] *Christian Baptist*, page 443.

Mr. Campbell was now recognized as the ablest representative of the Christian faith, and when his acceptance of Mr. Owen's challenge was made known, all felt that the Goliath of infidelity was now to meet his David.

It was arranged that the debate should take place in Cincinnati in April, 1829. The occasion was a great one. The reputation of the disputants had created widespread interest. Those who sympathized with Mr. Owen predicted a speedy overthrow of the Bible. Those who had heard Mr. Campbell felt that the cause of the Christian religion had fallen into good hands. The debate which followed brought out the strongest arguments of either side. Having at length exhausted his resources, Mr. Owen sat down, and Mr. Campbell was left to continue his argument without an opponent to reply, which he did in an address of twelve hours length upon the evidences of Christianity as a supernatural religion. It was at the close of this masterful defense of the Christian faith, that one not in sympathy with Mr. Campbell religiously, remarked: "I have been listening to a man who seems as one who had lived in all ages." Mr. Owen had hitherto exerted a poisonous influence in society unchecked, but in this discussion he was completely routed, and not long afterward abandoned his infidel schemes and returned to Scotland.

It was while arranging the preliminaries of this debate, that Mr. Owen visited Mr. Campbell at the Bethany mansion. During one of their excursions about the farm together, they came to the family burying-ground. Pausing for a moment among its tombs, Mr. Owen remarked:

"There is one advantage I have over the Christian,—I am not afraid to die. Most Christians have fear in death, but if some few items of my business were settled, I should be perfectly willing to die at any moment."

"Well," Mr. Campbell replied, "you say you have no fear in death; have you any hope in death?"

"No," said Mr. Owen, after a solemn pause.

"Then," rejoined Mr. Campbell, pointing to an ox standing nearby, "you are on a level with that brute. He has fed till he is satisfied, and stands in the shade whisking off the flies, and has neither hope nor fear in death."

It is related that after the debate Mr. Owen again accepted of the hospitality of his invincible antagonist, was treated by him with great kindness, and urged to abandon infidelity and accept Christ as a Savior. The appeal melted Mr. Owen to tears; he buried his face in his hands, but still clung to that which he could not sustain.

In this discussion Mr. Campbell did most valiant service for the cause of Christianity, and commanded the respect and admiration of the entire religious community, irrespective of party affiliation. For a time denominational differences were forgotten, and all were disposed to recognize in him a defender of the common faith. An effective check was put to the threatened spread of unbelief, and the debate, which was published, remained one of the strongest documents on Christian evidences, and is possibly the best reflection of the versatile mind of the great advocate of primitive Christianity in the zenith of his power.

His manly, courteous treatment of those who were skeptical, won the respect even of the professed enemies of Christianity. They flocked to hear him, were brought under conviction by his fair-minded, unsectarian presentation of the claims of revealed religion, and many of them became obedient to the Gospel. As an evidence of the appreciation with which he was regarded by this class, he was invited by the skeptics of New York to address them on two successive evenings in their own Tammany Hall, and met them with such suavity and power, as "to draw praise from every lip and secure a vote of thanks from the very men whose air-built castle he demolished."

Mr. Campbell had hardly finished correcting the proofs of his debate with Robert Owen, when he was called upon to encounter an enemy nearer home. Near the close of the year 1830, the Mormon delusion began its course in northern Ohio, and among its promoters was one of Mr. Campbell's lieutenants, Sydney Rigdon. Together with Joseph Smith he perpetrated the fraud of "The Lost Manuscript Found," which was published as the "Book of Mormon," and gathering a few credulous followers, organized them, on the basis of its teachings, into the

"Church of the Latter Day Saints." Taking advantage of his former connection with the reformatory work fostered by Mr. Campbell, Rigdon sought to lead away the churches of the vicinity in which he began his operations, and succeeded in making shipwreck of the cause in Kirtland, when Alexander Campbell paid a visit to that section of Ohio, exposed the shameless imposition, and put a stop to its progress, and soon had the satisfaction of witnessing the departure of Joseph Smith and his deluded followers to the regions beyond.

In the meantime, Mr. Campbell's energies were largely consumed in enlarging the borders and strengthening the defenses of the work now so auspiciously begun. At least six months of the year were spent away from home in extended tours, lecturing, preaching, organizing, and in endeavoring to supply that which was lacking in a newly-formed religious society. New churches were constantly being established. The plea for apostolic Christianity was springing up in unexpected quarters. Misrepresentation and bitter prejudice were to be met, errors to be corrected, order restored. In meeting the varied demands made upon him, he could say with Paul, "Besides those things that are without, that which cometh upon me daily, the care of all the churches."

Enlargement to the forces and influence of the Christian Church came, at this period, from another source. Earlier in his labors Mr. Campbell had come in touch with the leaders of a kindred movement, which had spread widely through the south. Its leading spirit was Barton W. Stone, formerly a Presbyterian minister. Like Mr. Campbell, he had turned from the Westminster Confession to the Bible, and had determined to accept, as his only guide in matters of religion, the Holy Scriptures. Like Mr. Campbell, he was led by its guidance to accept immersion as scriptural baptism, and to reject all human designations for the church, content with the simple name of *Christian*.

In 1824, during one of Mr. Campbell's tours in Kentucky, these two reformers met for the first time. Two such spirits could not but be interested in each other. Their aims were one, though they differed slightly in some of their conclusions and methods. A cordial, friendly investigation of their views was begun. At first, like Luther and Zwingli, they seemed to be separated by irreconcilable differences, but upon a closer inquiry these disappeared. The ultimate result we have in Mr. Stone's own words: "We plainly saw that we were on the same foundation, in the same spirit, and preached the same Gospel." Accordingly, in the early part of 1832, the two bodies united throughout Kentucky, thus materially strengthening the forces and influence of primitive Christianity in that State, and exemplifying their plea for the union of God's children.

In the autumn of 1836, Mr. Campbell was brought face to face with a religious antagonist from an entirely different quarter. In October of that year he had been invited to deliver an address before the College of Teachers of Cincinnati. As the public mind was already somewhat exercised by the attempt of the Catholic Church to exclude the Bible from the public schools, he chose for his subject "Moral Culture," ascribing the rapid march of modern civilization to the spirit of inquiry awakened by the Protestant Reformation. Bishop Purcell, a Roman Catholic prelate, took strong exceptions to Mr. Campbell's lecture, declaring that the "Protestant Reformation had been the cause of all the contention and infidelity in the world." Mr. Campbell was not the man to allow such a misstatement of facts to pass unchallenged; so he informed the bishop that he was prepared to defend the cause of Protestantism against such misrepresentation in public discussion. As the bishop failed to signify his acceptance of this proposition, Mr. Campbell delivered another address, presenting six propositions, which he declared himself able at any time to sustain.

So wrought up was the community over the attack of the Catholic Church upon American institutions, that its representative men did not feel disposed to let the matter end in that way. An appeal, signed by many of the prominent citizens of Cincinnati, was, therefore, presented to Mr. Campbell, urging him to a public exposure of the absurd claims and usages of the Roman Catholic Church, and to establish before the community the six propositions announced in his lecture. In reply, Mr. Campbell consented to sustain his position against Bishop Purcell, or any of the Catholic priesthood, providing only that time be allowed him to fulfill existing engagements.

It was finally arranged that a seven days' joint discussion should take place between Mr. Campbell and Bishop Purcell in Cincinnati, beginning on January 13, 1837. In this discussion, one of the most important in which he ever engaged, Mr. Campbell took the aggressive side in the seven propositions considered, maintaining that,

> *1. The Roman Catholic institution, sometimes called the Holy Apostolic Church, is not now nor was she ever catholic, apostolic or holy, but is a sect in the fair import of that word, older than any other sect now existing; not the mother and mistress of all churches, but an apostasy from the only true, apostolic and catholic Church of Christ.*
>
> *2. Her notion of apostolic succession is without any foundation in the Bible, in reason, or in fact; an imposition of the most injurious consequences, built upon unscriptural and antiscriptural traditions, resting wholly upon the opinions of interested and fallible men.*
>
> *3. She is not uniform in her faith or united in her members, but mutable and fallible as any other sect of philosophy or religion,—Jewish, Turkish, or Christian,—a confederation of sects under a politico-ecclesiastic head.*
>
> *4. She is the Babylon of John, the Man of Sin of Paul, and the Empire of the Youngest Horn of Daniel's sea-monster.*
>
> *5. Her notions of purgatory, indulgences, auricular confession, remission of sins, transubstantiation, supererogation, etc., essential elements of her system, are immoral in their tendency and injurious to the well-being of society, religious and political.*
>
> *6. Notwithstanding her pretensions to have given us the Bible and faith in it, we are perfectly independent of her for our knowledge of that book and its evidences of a divine original.*

> *7. The Roman Catholic religion, if infallible and
> unsusceptible of reformation, as alleged, is essentially
> anti-American, being opposed to the genius of all free
> institution, and positively subversive of them, oppos-
> ing the general reading of the Scriptures and the dif-
> fusion of useful knowledge among the whole commu-
> nity, so essential to liberty and the permanency of
> good government.[1]*

To this discussion Mr. Campbell brought his wonderful
researches and extensive acquaintance with the history of the
church, ancient and modern. His early observations in
priest-ridden Ireland, his inborn hatred of priestly arrogance,
his high ground of observation, which enabled him to look
beyond creed and party lines to a universal and untrammeled
brotherhood in Christ, fitted him, as no other man of his day, to
become the champion of Protestantism. A sentence or two in
his opening address reveal the grandeur of his purpose:

> *I appear before you at this time, in the good provi-
> dence of our Heavenly Father, in defense of the truth,
> and in explanation of the great redeeming, regener-
> ating, ennobling principles of Protestantism, as op-
> posed to the claims and pretensions of the Roman
> Catholic Church. I come not here to advocate the
> particular tenets of any sect, but to defend the great
> cardinal principles of Protestantism.[2]*

In the discussion which followed, Mr. Campbell sustained
his reputation and his cause to the satisfaction of the friends of
Protestantism of whatever creed, and won the warmest com-
mendation of all foes of Catholic arrogance. A public meeting
was called to voice the sentiment of the community. A series of
resolutions was unanimously passed, complimenting in the
highest terms Mr. Campbell's services, and declaring "that it is
the unanimous opinion of this meeting that the cause of Protestantism has been fully sustained throughout the discussion."

---

[1] *Campbell and Purcell Debate*, page 7.
[2] *Campbell and Purcell Debate*, page 8.

So deep and lasting was the impression of Mr. Campbell's defense of Protestantism and of an open and untrammeled Bible as the safeguard of the Republic, that at the next meeting of the College of Teachers at Cincinnati, a resolution was passed to the effect, "That in the judgment of the College, the Bible should be introduced into every school, from the lowest to the highest, as a text-book."

The debate was published, had an extensive sale, and presents, perhaps, the ablest defense of Protestantism in the English language. Himself the last great protestant against religious error, it was fitting that upon him should fall the responsibility of defending a cause that had been purchased by the best blood of modern civilization.

Chapter Eleven:
A WISE MASTER-BUILDER

We have witnessed, in these pages, the laying of the foundation of a religious movement deep and strong in the imperishable Word. Mr. Campbell had, from the beginning, insisted that every principle used in its construction should have the stamp of divine approval; and now it was his daily concern that the superstructure should, in ever particular, be worthy of the foundation. In securing results commensurate with his great undertaking, his energies were taxed to their utmost.

From 1836 to 1840 he traveled extensively, looking after the progress of the work over a wide field. During the summer of 1836 he made an extended tour through the East, where the principles of the reformation were as yet imperfectly understood, and where he was confronted by a spirit of conservatism that gave but feeble response to a plea, which, in the hospitable South and the enterprising West, was becoming a potent factor in religious society. From a flourishing town in New York he writes:

> *I have never been more busily engaged in all my life than on the present tour. I am like one settling in a new country, where everything is to do. I have labored incessantly since I came into this State, disabusing the public mind, and teaching the disciples. There is a powerful opposition consolidated against the truth... I am really very tired and willing to seek repose, and could wish that my journey and my furlough were completed, but I must patiently bear the toil and endure the pain in hope of the reward. I have the great pleasure of enlightening many, of relieving the distressed and broken in spirit, and of making some rich in the faith and hope of Christ. I have left a good odor for Christ in every place.*[1]

---

[1] *Memoirs of Alexander Campbell*, Vol. 2, page 415.

After bearing testimony to the truth in many cities of the East, he returned to his home among the hills of Virginia, having, during an absence of ninety-four days, traveled two thousand miles and delivered ninety-three discourses.

Having explored and discovered little promise for the cause of reformation in the eastern States, he turned his attention to the South. Already the cause had made remarkable progress in Virginia, Kentucky, and Tennessee. Beyond the borders of these States but feeble and ineffectual attempts had been made to establish reformatory principles. During a few months' tour, he visited the leading cities of the South, everywhere pleading with his accustomed power for the restoration of primitive Christianity. Of the reception of his plea he writes:

> *My present tour reminds me of those in 1823-25, when I was widely scattering the seeds of reformation in the West. The first principles of things—the objections of the captious, the scruples of the conscientious, the problems of the curious, and the ambushes of the enemies—all require and receive a degree of atten-tion. We have to dispossess demons, and exorcise unclean spirits, as well as to proclaim the acceptable year of the Lord. The chief priests, the scribes, and the rulers of the people are generally in league against us. But there are some more noble than in Thessalo-nica who hear the word with teachableness.[1]*

When, after many weary months of trial and labor, he again turned his steps homeward, it was in no spirit of optimism that he penned his conclusions. Sectarianism was strongly en-trenched in many quarters, and moral degeneracy pervaded religious society. "There is," he wrote, "everywhere more of a readiness to reform the creed than the heart, to rectify the un-derstanding rather than the affections, and to exhibit sound tenets rather than godly lives; good works are much more wanting than good notions. Millions are consumed upon the lusts of men for thousands that are laid up on deposit in the

---

[1] *Memoirs of Alexander Campbell*, Vol. 2, page 452.

Bank of Heaven."[1] While these tours, involving great labor and sacrifice on the part of Mr. Campbell, failed of large results, they were connected with an important enterprise that now consumed the thought and energy of the great leader. They had revealed to him the weakness of the cause of reformation. It was lack of men competent to carry forward the work. In the great conflict which fired his heart and brain, he had been compelled to use such material as presented itself to aid in the spread of the Gospel. Those who came to his support, were, many of them, untrained men from the farms and shops, who had entered the ministry of the Word without preparation, other than a study of the New Testament; and by their narrow and superficial conception of Christianity, often hindered rather than aided the progress of truth. Though always the friend of education, he became convinced, as at no former period of his life, that if his cause were to continue to prosper and commend itself to thinking people, it must be supported by an educated ministry. He, therefore, began seriously to consider the establishment of an institution where young men could secure training which would make them efficient advocates of the cause of primitive Christianity, now so widely spread; and whose talent, culture and acquaintance with the Word would command the respect, attention and acceptance of the world.

In the consideration of this problem, as in every other subject that came within the grasp of his intellect, Mr. Campbell took grounds that were far in advance of his times. He regarded it as a serious defect of a college training that so much time was devoted to the pagan classics, to the exclusion of the physical sciences and the study of the Christian Scriptures. He conceived an educational institution in which the physical, intellectual, moral, and religious constitution of man would each receive training. His system embraced, 1st, A family institution under the control of Christian people, where lads under fourteen could be brought together, and carefully instructed in the facts, precepts, and promises of the Bible, and trained up in the paths of morality and religion. 2nd. A school embracing a

---

[1] *Memoirs of Alexander Campbell*, Vol. 2, page 462.

complete course of preparation for college, in which the "formation of moral character and the culture of the heart was to be made the supreme end." 3rd. The college for which he proposed a liberal course of studies in which the physical sciences should have prominence. But he argued the importance of such instruction, even in classic halls, as would secure the development of the moral faculties as indispensable to correct views of life and society. Therefore, the Bible should, he insisted, be made one of the regular text-books, no student to be entitled to honors without being thoroughly acquainted with the Sacred Oracles. 4th. The church with which the institution was to be connected, presenting to the young men under its instruction, and to the world, a practical exhibition of the truth and excellency of the Gospel of Christ. By the employment of such a scheme, Mr. Campbell hoped to remedy the errors he had witnessed, and build upon the one foundation an enduring superstructure of moral and intellectual excellence. In announcing his purpose he said:

> *Having now completed fifty years and on my way to sixty, the greater part of which time I have been engaged in literary labors and pursuits, and imagining that I possess some views and attainments which I can in this way render permanently useful to this community and posterity, I feel in duty bound to offer this project to the consideration of all the friends of literature, morality, and unsectarian Bible Christianity.*[1]

Mr. Campbell's scheme of education being heartily approved, not only by his own brethren, but by eminent educators of various creeds, steps were at once taken to carry out its provisions. There was but one spot where such an experiment could be put in successful operation, and that was near the mansion of the sage whose wisdom and fame would assure it pre-eminence. A charter was consequently obtained for Bethany College during the winter of 1840, and a board of trustees selected, who at once chose Mr. Campbell president of the in-

---

[1] *Memoirs of Alexander Campbell*, Vol. 2, page 469.

stitution. With his characteristic energy, he immediately proceeded to secure buildings and funds, declaring his readiness to render his services without compensation and to invest a few thousand dollars besides, providing others would take hold and assist in building up an institution which should be made "a lasting and comprehensive blessing." So rapidly was the work prosecuted, that by October 21, 1841, the doors of Bethany College were opened for students. Mr. Campbell at once addressed himself to the work of training young men in the great principles of Divine truth. The sacred volume was made the text-book for the whole college, and every morning he proceeded to develop before all the students the great facts which it presented. At a later period, he was able to say:

> *From the origin of Bethany College till this day, a period of over sixteen years, there has been a Bible study and a Bible lecture for every college day in the college year. The Bible is read as it was written, in chronological order, and a lecture on every reading is delivered exegetical of its facts and documents—historical, chronological, geographical—whether they be natural, moral or religious, in reference to the past, the present, the future of man.[1]*

No feature of the institution over which he presided gave Mr. Campbell more satisfaction than this study of the Bible as one of the branches of a liberal education. "A college or school," said he, "adapted to the genius of human nature—to man as he is and as he must hereafter be—cannot be found in Christendom, in the absence of a moral education founded upon the Bible, and the Bible alone, without the admixture of human speculation, or of science falsely so-called." But strange as it may seem, of the one hundred and more colleges in the United States in 1841, Bethany alone had a chair of Sacred and Biblical Literature.

The first half of each college session was devoted to the study of the Pentateuch, and the last half to the four Gospels

---

[1] *Home Life*, page 61.

and the Acts of the Apostles. Mr. Campbell's morning lectures on the Pentateuch before the students of Bethany College revealed him at his best. Under his magic treatment the pages of Holy Writ beamed with new meaning, and a new and widespread interest was awakened in its study. The great motive which prompted him to superadd to his already oppressive labors the additional responsibility of Bethany College, was to "magnify the value of this book of books,—to enforce its claims to authority over the heart and consciences of men,—to expound its great and eternal principles of righteousness and truth—and to make men feel that it is the word of the living God, the Divine standard of truth in religion and of virtue in morality."

The influence of Bethany College, from the very beginning of its history, proved the wisdom of its founder. It was soon able to send out talented and educated preachers, who gave new impetus to the cause of the Reformation, and at a critical period in the history of the movement saved it from the narrow, sectarian channels into which well-meaning but ignorant men would have drifted it. Other institutions of learning, dominated by the same supreme regard for the Word of God, sprang up under the influence of the educational spirit which Mr. Campbell's wisdom and foresight had created, and already the foundation has been laid for the Disciples of Christ to take their place in the front rank of the world's educators.

In one respect Mr. Campbell's comprehensive scheme of education proved a disappointment. It was a cherished notion of his that the best results in college education could be attained by gathering the youth from their homes, and putting them under early moral training and instruction, preparatory to a college course. To carry out his design he erected, at his own expense, a large building near the college, where the family school could be put in operation. It was soon discovered, however, that young boys, away from the influence of home and parental guardianship, were peculiarly exposed, and failing to find persons suitably qualified for the management of such a charge, it was reluctantly abandoned; though Mr. Campbell still cherished the belief that under proper direction his highest hopes might have been attained.

While immersed in the cares and labors attendant upon the inauguration of his great educational enterprise, Mr. Campbell was again called upon to defend the ground which he had taken in another public discussion.

Already he had proved himself the ablest champion of revealed religion in America. When Robert Owen challenged the clergy of the world, and posted his defiance on the walls of our cities, Mr. Campbell met him in a public debate, which put a check to his infidel schemes in this country. In his debate with Bishop Purcell, he successfully attacked the arrogant and hollow pretensions of Roman Catholicism. In this last encounter he was called upon to defend the religion of the New Testament against the traditions and other baseless tenets of Protestantism.

In the fall of 1842, while on a visit to Kentucky, Mr. Campbell had received an intimation that the Presbyterians of that state were ready to furnish a champion in the public discussion of the points of difference between them and the Disciples of Christ. Mr. Campbell promptly declared his readiness to defend his views against any of their representative men. Dr. R. J. Breckenridge, a man of fine attainments and excellent Christian spirit, was looked upon as the best representative of the Presbyterian cause; but when solicited to engage Mr. Campbell in debate, he answered: "No sir, I will never be Alexander Campbell's opponent. A man who has done what he has to defend Christianity against infidelity, and to defend Protestantism against the delusions and usurpations of Catholicism, I will never oppose in public debate. I esteem him too highly."[1] At length, Rev. N. L. Rice was chosen by the Presbyterians, and after a lengthy correspondence the propositions and terms of discussion were agreed upon. The ground of debate on this occasion had somewhat shifted from that of Mr. Campbell's earlier encounters with the Presbyterian clergy. It was no longer a contest between Baptists and Pedo-baptists, but between Reformers, then, as now, called Christians or Disciples of Christ, and the religious world. The subjects under discus-

---

[1] *Millennial Harbinger*, 1866, page 200.

sion covered the whole range of truth for which the Disciples contended. The following propositions were finally agreed upon:

1. The immersion in water of a proper subject, into the name of the Father, the Son, and the Holy Spirit, is the one, only apostolic or Christian baptism. Mr. Campbell affirms.

2. The infant of a believing parent is a scriptural subject of baptism. Mr. Rice affirms.

3. Christian baptism is for the remission of past sins. Mr. Campbell affirms.

4. Baptism is to be administered only by a bishop or ordained presbyter. Mr. Rice affirms.

5. In conversion and sanctification, the Spirit of God operates on persons only through the word of truth. Mr. Campbell affirms.

6. Human creeds, as bonds of union and communion, are necessarily heretical and schismatical. Mr. Campbell affirms.[1]

In every instance, Mr. Campbell advocated and defended the simple requirements of the Gospel as he found them in the New Testament, against ecclesiastical theories and practices as presented by creeds and confessions of faith. Lexington was selected as the place of discussion, and Henry Clay, the great Kentucky orator and statesman, was chosen to preside; and here for a period of eighteen days, beginning November 15, 1843, was waged one of the greatest intellectual battles of religious history.

In some respects this was Mr. Campbell's most unsatisfactory effort, in some respects his greatest. The difference between the disputants was marked, both as to their mental characteristics and modes of warfare. Mr. Campbell's mind was of that comprehensive type, broad in its generalizations, capable of grasping at the fundamental principles of the subject under consideration, and carrying his point by an intellectual

---

[1] *Campbell and Rice Debate*, page 47.

momentum that was irresistible when launched at his antagonist. Mr. Rice, on the other hand, though lacking in Mr.
Campbell's power of thought, possessed an intellectual agility
that was able to parry the thrusts of his opponent by grasping at
the exceptions and hurling them back with effect. As viewed
from the standpoint of one of Mr. Rice's sympathizers, "Mr.
Campbell was like a heavy, Dutch- built man-of-war, carrying
many guns of large caliber; while Mr. Rice resembled a daring
and active Yankee privateer, who contrived, by the liveliness of
his movements and the ease with which he could take up his
position for a raking fire, to leave his more cumbrous adversary
in a very crippled condition at the close of the fight." Great
abilities were displayed by both parties in this discussion.
While Mr. Rice claimed complete victory for his side, the ultimate effect of the debate upon religious society did not justify
the claim. A copyright of the printed debate, which filled more
than nine hundred closely printed pages, was purchased by a
member of the Presbyterian Church, and the volume was circulated for a time as a defense of their views. But it was soon
discovered that its effect upon the public mind was quite different from what its publisher expected, and that it was making
many converts to Mr. Campbell's views, and none to Mr.
Rice's. Consequently the copyright was disposed of to a
member of the Christian Church, under whose auspices it was
widely circulated, and with good effect, in disseminating their
views.

Whatever may be said against this mode of presenting and
defending the truth today, it was made in Mr. Campbell's
hands, and under the conditions of society prevailing at that
time, a powerful instrument in stirring up the spirit of earnest
investigation. In his attack and defeat of the foes of Christianity, he has contributed in no small measure to the growth of
respect for the Bible and its institutions. In his championship of
the cause of Protestantism, he presented a much needed check
to Catholic presumption; while in his advocacy of the Bible
against creeds and confessions, he has rendered invaluable aid
to the triumph of the simple claims of the Gospel. Thus did he
seek to enlarge the Church of Christ into harmonious propor-

tion with the Divine foundation upon which it was established; and, as a wise master-builder, to rear a Temple of Faith, whose strength and grandeur should be unsurpassed, and whose beauty should be enduring.

Chapter Twelve:
THE PRINCE OF PREACHERS

While much of Mr. Campbell's strength and energy was consumed in educational and editorial labors, he was first and last and all the time a preacher of the Gospel. From the moment when, sitting on the stump of a broken mast of a shipwrecked vessel, he dedicated his life to the ministry of the Word, to the time when he stepped down from the Bethany pulpit never to return, on account of the infirmities of age, he did not once swerve from his calling.

Perhaps no point in his career will furnish us a better eminence from which to study the character and secret of his great power as a preacher than that at which we have now arrived,—his fame world- wide, his powers unabated by the decay of age.

Able as a writer, painstaking and inspiring as a teacher, he was seen at his best in the pulpit. Here as he developed the great themes of Christ and Redemption, he never failed to surprise and delight all who came under the sound of his voice. Here his power was irresistible. Men who came to criticize, returned to praise. Even those most bitterly opposed to his views were compelled to bear testimony to his extraordinary power as a speaker. Ministers exhorted their flocks to refuse him hearing, lest they should be swept from their religious moorings by his irresistible logic. It is not strange, therefore, that his friends regarded him with unmixed admiration, and cherished it as the supreme moment of their lives when permitted to sit under the charmed influence of his persuasive voice.

It is impossible to convey to the printed page any adequate conception of Mr. Campbell as a preacher. He was not a sermon writer, and nothing but the barest outlines of a few of his sermons have been preserved. But even if we now possessed his discourses in full, they would fail to reveal the secret of the spell the great preacher was able to throw about his auditors. There is an element in the public address which, like the fragrance of the flower, cannot be preserved. The thoughts remain, but the personality of the thinker is gone. Our knowledge of one whose voice has long been silenced must come from those who have felt the power of his eloquence; and in Mr. Campbell's case even his hearers are removed a generation from us, only here and there some veteran remaining who can tell us how he preached in the greatness of his prime.

In the very beginning of his ministry he revealed a rare power of thought and utterance which was prophetic of the commanding position which he speedily attained. He was blessed by nature with an attractive personality. Before he uttered a word all eyes were fixed upon him with an expectation that was never disappointed. He was endowed with a mind of extraordinary keenness and grasp, whose furnishing had not been neglected, and whose power of memory, observation, and generalization had been cultivated to a high degree of perfection by long and painstaking effort. He had mastered the one book which was to furnish the material and inspiration of his preaching. Like Timothy, he had known the Holy Scriptures from his youth; and like that young disciple, he made it his constant study to show himself approved unto God, rightly dividing the Word. The charm of his discourse was multiplied by a rich endowment of voice, whose low, musical tones were in keeping with the sublime message which fell from the lips of the speaker. Back of it all was an intense earnestness of purpose, which is ever indispensable to a powerful presentation of the Gospel message. He loved the Bible with an intense, passionate love. "This," he would say, pointing to the Word of God, "is perfect, and I fall a martyr ere the profane finger of mortal shall smut it or change it." He could say with Paul, "We also believe, therefore we speak."

His method of presenting the truth was altogether novel and original. "He thought as no other man ever thought, spoke as no other man ever spoke, wrote as no other man ever wrote." As multitudes dispersed after listening for the first time to his presentation of the Gospel claims, they were constrained to remark, "We never heard it in this like before."

With his peculiar capacity for generalization, he was able to grasp and present the essential and vital principles of revelation in wide and expanded views. But if the view was sublime in its breadth and grandeur, it was nevertheless clear and simple in its detail. At a time when the authorized clergy were claiming that the Scriptures were beyond the power of the ordinary understanding, Mr. Campbell was demonstrating that the simplicity of the Gospel brought its truths within the reach of all. At his bidding doctrines that had long been obscured by the mists of tradition suddenly emerged from the enveloping clouds, like the landscape from the morning mists which the rising sun has scattered.

The burden of his discourses was to show what the Divine Word says and why it is said. Instead of confining himself to the development of a single passage, he would sweep the horizon of Revelation in his survey, unfolding in its light the lesson of a chapter, a book, or a dispensation, its meaning illumined and enforced by a wealth of scriptural illustration and authority. After listening for more than two hours to one of his discourses on the Epistle to the Galatians, a Baptist minister, who regarded Mr. Campbell with suspicion, was heard to remark, "I know nothing about him, but be he devil or saint, he has thrown more light on that epistle and the whole Scriptures than I have heard in all the sermons I ever listened to before." James Madison, ex-President of the United States, after bearing testimony as to Alexander Campbell's ability and services in the constitutional convention of his State, continued: "But it is as a theologian that Mr. Campbell must be known. It was my privilege to hear him very often as a preacher of the Gospel, and I regard him as the ablest and most original expounder of the Word I have ever heard."

In manner Mr. Campbell used none of the artificial accessories of oratory. "Of the artificial," says one intimately acquainted him, "he had not one vestige in him. He had it neither in his look nor in his talk, in his writing nor in anything else. Never was man freer from the influence of mere conventionalities." As one remarked of him, he had no time to study gesture and cultivate himself in the graces of oratory. Life rushed on too fast; so he passed these by and addressed himself to the understanding of his hearers, in the best, most forcible English he could command.

Trusting in the power of great truths clearly and earnestly presented to produce convictions, he usually delivered his address without movement, or attempt at eloquence. He seemed rather to despise oratory as an art, always relying on the inherent attractiveness of the truths he uttered. His utterances were rapid, sometimes too rapid for the listener to keep pace with the torrent of ideas that flowed on in an endless stream. He usually talked in conversational style, with scarcely a gesture from the beginning to the end of his discourse. But there was a dignity of bearing, a charm of manner, a clearness of statement, a force of reasoning, a purity of diction, a wealth of learning and an earnestness of purpose, which "clothed his pulpit efforts with a high degree of oratorical excellence."

He always spoke without notes, but not without preparation. In his earlier efforts this consisted in carefully writing and memorizing his entire address, but when once he felt confident of his powers, he trusted to the fertile resources of his great intellect to marshal at his command fact and argument and illustration, with which to bring the truth home with conviction to the hearts of his hearers. When asked how he possessed himself of such a vast store-house of information with which he illumined his discourse, he replied, "By studying sixteen hours per day." Indeed, his mind seemed never to have been released from the great theme to which he had devoted his life. Whether in the study, or behind the plow, or on his way to some distant appointment, or within the charmed circle about his own fireside, his mind dwelt upon the mysteries of redeeming love. "Many a piece of a day he spent wandering beside his winding Buffalo, or clambering over its neighboring woody slopes. Here often seated on a log, or perched like a wild mountain bird on some lone rock, he would pass unconscious hours deep wrapped in thought, or searching the meaning of some dark text in his Greek Testament." Thus was forged and polished the weapon which he wielded with terrible effect against the enemies of his Lord.

As a preacher, he rose above environment in his enthusiasm for the truth. He seemed untouched by those circumstances which inspire other speakers to their loftiest flights. There were no great occasions in his life, because all occasions were to him equally great. It did not matter whether he spoke to a dozy congregation of half a hundred in the backwoods, or addressed an assembly of orators and statesmen in the halls of legislation, he was sure to rise to a height that was the wonder and the admiration of all who heard. In either case it was not the praise of men that he sought, but the approval of Him whose servant he was.

At a period when the ministers of religion were distinguished by clerical airs, clerical voice, clerical manners, clerical dress, Mr. Campbell appeared in refreshing contrast, which doubtless gave an added charm to his address. There was nothing of the clergyman about him. "Nature had not made him one, and he could never assume the character. It is but just to add that he never tried. His religion was a religion of principle, of conviction. In it was nothing conventional. Hence he never impressed the world as trying to seem clerical. He had neither clerical airs, nor a clerical gait. He neither walked like one, nor talked like one, and as he never seemed to be one, few people, not knowing him, ever suspected him for one."[1]

His place and power as a preacher has been assigned with discrimination by D. S. Burnett, in an address delivered before the students of Bethany College shortly after the close of Mr. Campbell's career. He says:

> *Mr. Campbell was a remarkable preacher. Not an orator, such as Whitfield, Summerfield, or the Irish Kirwan. He had not the voice, gesture, or pathos of either of them. He could not, like them, raise a storm and quell it at will; and yet he would draw a large congregation, hold them longer, and leave them furnished with much more comprehensive views of truth and duty. He spoke more sensibly, more rhetorically, and more scripturally than either of them, and his work on earth will abide longer. We can imagine few*

---

[1] *Lard's Quarterly*, Vol. 3, page 257.

more pleasurable sights than this grand preacher, delivering an extempore discourse, while supporting himself, enfeebled by dyspepsia, on his cane, in the midst of the largest and most intellectual audiences our country could afford. Thus he stood, like Paul on Mars' Hill, among the orators and statesmen of Kentucky, at an early day, in the largest hall of Lexington; thus he entranced the elite of Richmond in 1830, and of Nashville shortly after; thus, shortly before that, he held spell-bound for two hours the Legislature of Ohio, before breakfast ready to depart; it was thus, in 1833, he addressed, with great power, the skeptics of New York, two successive evenings, in their own Tammany Hall, with such suavity as to draw praise from every lip and secure a vote of thanks from the men whose air-built castle he demolished. These speeches flowed from his lips like the water from the rock smitten by the prophet, and the people felt, like famished Israel as they drank the cooling draught, that a hand of power had relieved their thirst. All were charmed with the man and impressed with the majesty of the Scriptures.[1]

To this should be added the following testimony of Dr. Richardson, his life-long friend and biographer:

For the first few moments, indeed, the hearer might contemplate his commanding form, his perfect self-posses- sion, and quiet dignity of manner, or admire the clear and silvery tones of his voice, but those emphatic tones soon filled his mind with other thoughts. New revelations of truth; themes the most familiar invested with a strange importance, as unexpected and yet obvious relations were developed in a few simple sentences; unthought of combinations; unforeseen conclusions; a range of vision that seemed to embrace the universe, and to glance at pleasure

---

[1] *Millennial Harbinger*, 1866, page 317.

into all its varied departments,—were as by some magic power presented to the hearer, and so as to wholly engross his perception and his understanding. While that voice was heard nothing could dissolve the charm.[1]

Like the preacher described in Dryden's lines,

With eloquence innate his tongue was arm'd,
Though harsh the precept, yet the preacher charm'd;
For letting down the golden chain from high,
He drew his audience upward to the sky.
He bore his great commission in his look,
And sweetly temper'd awe, and soften'd all he spoke.

It will thus be observed that Mr. Campbell possessed a power all his own. If it lacked in some of the graces of oratory, it was, nevertheless, adapted to the times and place he was providentially called to fill. Vast audiences were chained by it for hours, forgetful of everything but the message. So rapt was the attention that at the close of an address of two or three hours' length, his congregations were often surprised and disappointed when he announced his conclusion, thinking that he had only spoken a few minutes. Men who once heard him never forgot the peculiar exaltation experienced while under the spell of his eloquence. Said one who in his youth had listened to a discourse delivered by Mr. Campbell on the Hebrew letter: "It has been forty years since I heard that discourse, but it is as vivid in my memory, I think, as when I first heard it." In listening to him, all not only felt that they were in the presence of a great man, but that the message which he was delivering bore an indispensable relation to their well-being.

---

[1] *Memoirs of Alexander Campbell*, Vol. 2, page 583.

Chapter Thirteen:
TRAVELS AT HOME AND ABROAD

With the weight of increasing years and of increasing cares, Mr. Campbell had hoped to find release from the pain of protracted absence from home. He longed to spend his remaining years within the quiet of his own beloved Bethany, and in the development of the college which he looked upon as the crowning work of his life.

This fond dream was not to be realized. The burden of securing buildings, equipments, and endowment for the new college rested upon him. While friends were ready to contribute to its support, so great was the desire of the public to see and hear him, that they made a visit from Mr. Campbell the condition of their donations to the funds of the college. In addition, therefore, to his labors as editor and instructor, he was compelled to make extended tours that took him through all sections of the country, and in which he was everywhere received with open arms by admiring multitudes. A great change had taken place in public sentiment since those early days when he stood alone as the representative of an unpopular cause. Papers that then had sought his defamation, now treated him with respect and consideration. Cities and legislative halls received him as an honored guest, and sought from him a public expression of his views. Everywhere he was treated with a consideration due his distinguished ability. In these tours he did much to strengthen the hearts of the brethren and set in order the things that were lacking.

In the winter of 1843, Mr. Campbell visited the large cities of the East in the interests of the college, securing valuable contributions in money and scientific apparatus. But the South, in some respects, presented the most fruitful field at that time. Its own lack of educational facilities led it to seek for its young men the advantages of Northern institutions of learning. Its large fortunes, accumulated by means of remunerative slave labor, were dispensed with somewhat lavish hand on any educational system which would not endanger its own institution of slavery. It, therefore, happened that Mr. Campbell was encouraged to make repeated visits among the scattered and wealthy disciples of the Southern States, in canvassing for funds to build and enlarge Bethany College. .

It was during these tours through the South that Mr. Campbell became personally acquainted with the evils of American slavery, and formulated for himself a course, which, in the light of our new birth of freedom, can hardly be justified. While recognizing and acknowledging the evil of this system which had fastened itself on a large section of our country, he was slow to recognize the righteousness of the cause of emancipation. While an anti-slavery man himself, he felt that the Bible under certain conditions justified slavery, and with him the authority of the Word of God was final on any question. While Wendell Philips was thundering his philippics against this stronghold of injustice, Mr. Campbell was penning his convictions for the columns of the *Harbinger*, declaring:

> *1. That the relation of master and servant is not in itself sinful or immoral. 2. That, nevertheless, slavery, as practiced in any part of the civilized world, is inexpedient, because not in harmony with the spirit of the age, nor the moral advancement of society... 3. That no Christian community, governed by the Bible, Old Testament and New, can constitutionally and rightfully make the simple relation of master and slave a term of Christian fellowship.* [1]

Before we pronounce judgment against Mr. Campbell for his apparent indifference to the sufferings of four million bondsmen, let us remember that he kept company with the great thinkers and teachers of the Christian denominations at that time. The Rev. Wilbur Fisk, the leader of New England Methodism, declared that "the general rule of Christianity not only permits, but in supposable circumstances enjoins a continuance of the master's authority." Dr. Wayland, the distinguished president of Brown University and leader of the Baptist

---

[1] *Millennial Harbinger*, 1845, page 263.

hosts, taught that "the people of the North are in such relation to the people of the South that they ought not to agitate the question of slavery, and that it would be an act of bad faith for Congress to abolish slavery in the District of Columbia." S. Irenaeus Prime declared in the *New York Observer*, as late as 1858, that the suppression of anti-slavery sentiment in the American Tract Society was "the greatest moral victory of truth over error achieved since the reformation of Martin Luther." Thus the various parties of religious society "wide apart as the poles, and swearing prayers at one another on other points, were cordially at one on this."

It is perhaps in some respects unjust to the memory of Mr. Campbell to associate his name with this company. For he recognized the evils of slavery and believed that it should give way before the growing spirit of humanity and the moral advancement of society. But his call from God was not the breaking of the temporal shackles of an enslaved race, but the spiritual emancipation of an enslaved world. With a few passing observations, therefore, upon the question which was agitating the public mind, he turned his mind to the completion of the task that for more than a quarter of a century had consumed his energies, allowing that no element of discord should interfere with the re-establishment of the primitive Gospel among men. His conservatism involved him, as we shall soon see, in no little trouble; but it is perhaps due to his course that, in those days of conflict that rent asunder great ecclesiastical bodies, there was no Christian Church North and Christian Church South, but one Christian Church both North and South.

So favorably had the cause progressed at home under his wise direction, that in 1847 he felt justified in gratifying the long-cher- ished desire of revisiting his native land. Though nearly forty years had elapsed since he had left the island that gave him birth, he was by no means a stranger to the English speaking people beyond the Atlantic. The *Christian Baptist* and his published debates had already preceded him, and had not been without recognition and fruit in many sections of Great Britain. Churches, reproducing the essential features of the

Christian churches in America, had sprung up in many quarters of England and Scotland. Pressing invitations, which now came to him from these churches, assuring him of a cordial reception, induced him to undertake the journey, which, but for an unfortunate circumstance, would have marked the happiest period of his life. From the day he landed at Liverpool he was constantly engaged in addressing large assemblies, and both in public and private explaining his religious tenets to interested listeners. In Liverpool Mr. Campbell was permitted to speak in a large hall, built by the followers of his former antagonist in debate, Robert Owen, for the promotion of infidelity, but then used for the defense and advancement of the Christianity it had been built to overthrow. In London he spoke frequently, once addressing a gathering of skeptics on the inspiration of the Christian Scriptures. Here he availed himself of the courtesies shown him by Mr. Bancroft, the American Minister, and other men of distinction, to see and hear the celebrities of the metropolis, in Parliament and church, and to visit her palaces and places of interest. While he saw much that pleased and charmed him, his heart went back to the quiet and comforts of his own sequestered home. In a letter to his daughter Clarinda, at the close of his London visit, he writes:

> *Meantime I sigh for repose, and often think of the hills around Bethany, and of the enviable lot of those I left behind me, compared to that of the millions through which I am passing in this Old World of palaces and hovels, of princes and beggars, of exuberant wealth and cheerless poverty. May the Lord in his mercy watch over your native country and long preserve it from the vices and follies which have entailed on France, on England, and on Europe an inheritance of miseries and misfortunes, from which the wisdom of politicians and the benevolence of Christians cannot rescue them for generations to come.[1]*

A hasty visit to Paris, which he viewed with mingled feel-

---

[1] *Memoirs of Alexander Campbell*, Vol. 2, page 549.

ings of astonishment and disgust, as he witnessed unrivaled splendor on the one hand, and beheld the most degrading religious mummeries on the other; a brief call at Cambridge and Oxford, those ancient and splendid seats of learning, which possessed for him an absorbing interest; a short sojourn at Manchester, with its mighty industries and wretched operatives—he continued his journey into Scotland without interruption or discomfort, tempering his holiday by an almost continuous sermon, in public or in private, upon the great theme of human redemption.

In Scotland, as in the earlier years of his labors at home, he became the victim of no little annoyance and persecution. Upon his arrival at Edinburgh he was involved in an unfortunate controversy with a local anti-slavery society, which gave a pretext to religious bigotry and led to some unhappy consequences. A few ministers, animated by dislike for his religious views, and fearing to engage him in open discussion, sought, as a means of weakening his influence, to excite against him public odium. As it was known that he was from Virginia, a slave State, nothing seemed so well suited to their purpose as to turn the anti-slavery sentiment of Scotland against him. A committee, under the guise of friendly visitors, waited upon him. To them he candidly stated the views which we have already discovered him to have held, making no concealment of his disapproval of the course pursued by abolitionists in Great Britain and America. In a few hours after this visit the city was billed with placards in large capitals, which ran as follows:

Citizens of Edinburgh—Beware! Beware! The Rev. Alexander Campbell of Virginia, United States of America, has been a slaveholder himself, and is still a defender of mansteaters!

Not satisfied with this attempt to check the growing influence of Mr. Campbell in Scotland, Rev. James Robertson, the leader of the crusade which was now inaugurated against him, challenged him to debate his position in regard to slavery. Having no time for oral debate, Mr. Campbell had to content himself by refuting the calumnious charges that were made against him in a public address, giving in full his views on the subject of American slavery, and hastened on to fulfill his engagements in other cities. The manner in which he was treated by the Scotch Anti-Slavery Society may be gathered from the following, published in the leading journal of Paisley, where he was announced to speak:

> *We beg to warn our readers against countenancing a Rev. or Mr. A. Campbell, of Virginia, U.S., who has announced a course of lectures in the Baptist chapel here. He is the apologist of man-stealing in its worst form—the advocate of all that is monstrous in that most monstrous of all systems—American slavery! Let the liberty-loving, slavery-despising people of Paisley repel from their precincts with the scowl of their worst displeasure, the apologist of American murderers, and let them show that they despise the advocate of man-stealing all the more because he comes clothed in the garb of sanctity.[1]*

Finding himself pursued by misrepresentation and abuse at every turn, Mr. Campbell at last addressed a letter to the *Edinburgh Journal*, consenting to an oral discussion of his position in regard to American slavery with anyone whom the Anti-Slavery Society might appoint, agreeing to meet "even Mr. Robertson himself, provided only that he were not that Rev. James Robertson (there being three ministers of that name in Edinburgh) who was publicly censured and excluded from the Baptist Church for violating the fifth commandment, with reference to his mother."

Continuing his tour through Scotland, he found himself once more on the streets of Glasgow, where as a young man he had spent one of the happiest years of his life. He had left the University nearly forty years before, an unknown student, and a radical religious dissenter, going out from his religious home in the bosom of Presbyterianism, and like Abraham, "not knowing

---

[1] *Millennial Harbinger*, 1848, page 50.

whither he went." Upon his return to these old scenes he was honored as the leader of a great religious movement, and constant demand was made upon him to hear more of the doctrine which he preached. While in the midst of these pleasant and profitable experiences, a warrant was served upon him at the instance of Rev. James Robertson, to prevent him from leaving Scotland, and claiming damages to the amount of five thousand pounds for alleged defamation of character. Pending his trial Mr. Campbell was offered his liberty on furnishing security for two hundred pounds. Friends rushed to his relief with the desired amount, which he promptly refused, choosing to go to prison until his cause could be heard and his arrest proved unwarranted and illegal.

> *I felt myself persecuted for righteousness' sake, and I could not find in my heart to buy myself off from imprisonment by tendering the required security. I thought it might be of great value to the cause of my Master if I should give myself into the hands of my persecutors, and thus give them an opportunity of showing their love of liberty, of truth, of righteousness by the treatment of myself in the relations I sustain to mankind as a Christian and a Christian teacher.*

For ten days he suffered the inconvenience and hardships of imprisonment. Though cast down, he was not forsaken, for friends vied with each other in ministering to his comfort, and letters poured in upon him from everywhere, expressing the kindliest sympathy. As soon as the matter could be brought before the court he was acquitted of the charge made against him, and permitted to continue his tour. But his friends, not satisfied to have the matter drop with his release from jail, brought suit against his chief persecutor for false imprisonment, and secured a judgment of ten thousand dollars in Mr. Campbell's favor, to avoid the payment of which Mr. Robertson thought proper to abscond; though with characteristic magnanimity Mr. Campbell had declared beforehand that should damages be awarded him he would not accept them.

After a tour through Ireland, shortened by the delays of his imprisonment, Mr. Campbell again turned his face homeward, arriving at Boston on Oct. 19, 1847. His reflections upon nearing the shore of the land of his adoption he thus records:

> *We can desire for ourselves no better political or temporal birthright or inheritance than we now possess, and we can pray for no greater honors or privileges of this world for any living people, greater or better than those guaranteed by our institution to every American citizen. May we act worthy of them!*

The joy which he experienced at homecoming, after an absence of several months, was speedily turned into sorrow by the announcement of the death of his second son, Wickliffe, a promising lad of ten, by drowning; but, as upon other occasions, he met affliction with a resignation and fortitude that attested the power of his religious convictions. He reverently submitted to the will of God, declaring: "He is too wise to err, and too kind causelessly to afflict the children of men."

His return from abroad was marked by renewal of zeal and effort in behalf of Bethany College. From editorial labors and college duties he frequently tore himself away, and took extended tours among his friends to secure funds to establish Bethany on a permanent basis. These pilgrimages had, notwithstanding the fatigue they occasioned, come to be numbered among the pleasant experiences of his life, for everywhere he was meeting old friends, who had shared with him the labors and odium of inaugurating and defending an unpopular movement. In the winter of 1849 he revisited Kentucky, where he was cheered and encouraged at every turn by the old veterans who had supported him and the cause of reformation in the days of small things. Thus the stages of his journey were punctuated by pleasant evenings with John T. Johnson, John A. Gano, John Smith, John Rodgers, Walter Scott, L. L. Pinkerton, and others by whose talents and energy the movement had been made popular throughout the State.

In the spring of 1850, while in the vicinity of Washington, D.C., he received a pressing invitation from both Houses of

Congress to deliver an address in the Capitol on the second of June. It is doubtful if such a scene has ever been witnessed in our National Capitol before or since. The House of Representatives was filled to overflowing. Here, after a hymn and prayer, Mr. Campbell was introduced, and addressed the assembly from John 3:17, "exhibiting the divine philanthropy in contrast with patriotism and human friendship, reasoning in a grand and masterly manner from creation, providence, divine legislation, and human redemption, and holding the audience in the most fixed attention during the time of the address, which occupied an hour and a half."

Near the close of this busy year Mr. Campbell wrote,

I have recently returned from a tour of forty days to Ohio, Kentucky, and Indiana, during which I traveled over sixteen hundred miles and delivered some thirty-eight discourses, besides as many long conversations. Fatigued, exhausted, worn out, I feel like one that has violated the first commandment of human nature— self-preservation. Before this, after one week's stay at home, I had been to New York and East twenty-four days, traveled fourteen hundred miles, and made some eight discourses—in all sixty-four days, three thousand miles and forty- six discourses.[1]

Never was father more devoted to the child of his old age, than was Mr. Campbell to the institution of learning which he planted and fostered as the last achievement of his fruitful life.

Bethany College has paramount claims on me and on all the friends of the cause to which I have consecrated my life. To further it abroad and build it up at home, in raising up men for the field when I shall be absent from this planet, seems to me a paramount duty. We have already in the field some of its first-fruits, and they are an offering most acceptable to the aggregate of all who hear them. We want a

---

[1] *Memoirs of Alexander Campbell*, Vol. 2, page591.

thousand men in the field of the world and another thousand in the vineyard of the Lord, preachers worthy of the Gospel and of the age, and teachers worthy of the Bible and of the church.

In seeking these results he continued his journey.

Chapter Fourteen:
THE BETHANY HOME

Any study of Alexander Campbell would be incomplete which did not introduce the reader to that charmed circle that gathered around the fireside at the Bethany mansion, with Mr. Campbell as its central figure; and at no period was it more inviting than in the halcyon days of life's autumn at which we have now arrived, and just before the gloom of winter had thrown its melancholy over the scene. For fifty years and more this home on the Buffalo, far away from the great marts of trade and centers of literature and fashion, was the moral center of the movement of which its distinguished occupant was the exponent.

The inner life of all noted men will not bear inspection. Magnanimous, chivalrous, generous in their public capacity, wife and children have found little to admire or respect or enjoy in their domestic relations. The lion of the arena has degenerated into the bear of the fireside, and home and family have felt the withering blight of an unlovely and unsympathetic nature. But this was not true of the home of Alexander Campbell. It reflected a warmth and a radiance that set off his religious sincerity in a charming light, and revealed the tenderer side of his nature.

Men who knew him only through his essays in the *Christian Baptist,* or the reputation given him by his religious enemies, were surprised by the geniality of his nature in social intercourse, and prejudice and resentment melted away as they met him face to face, as the winter's snows before the advancing season.

Those who knew Mr. Campbell best unite in their praise of the peculiar charm of his fireside fellowship. His hospitality was unbounded and administered with a freeness and familiarity that at once put his guests at their ease. As his field of influence broadened, and his fame spread through the surrounding States, his home was seldom without visitors, and the family meal seldom eaten alone. They came from every quarter to praise or to blame, to seek the truth or defend error, and all were cordially received and entertained with princely grace. These occasions were always made in some way to serve the cause to which he had devoted his energies; and the early advocates of the cause of reformation were won, not so much by his masterly discourses, as by friendly intercourse, in which his matchless conversational powers were irresistible. It is related that one afternoon two Baptist ministers, who had ridden on horseback more than a day's journey, drew up their horses before his house. They had learned of him through his debate with Walker, and came to hear from him more of the work of reform which he was inaugurating. A cordial welcome was extended to them, and after tea a conversation, or, rather, monologue, for it was Mr. Campbell that did the talking, began, which continued through the entire night, and ended in winning them as firm friends and efficient champions of the movement to restore the primitive faith.

He was a gifted conversationalist, and nowhere was that gift displayed to greater advantage than at his own fireside. One who often sat under its spell has thus written:

> *In conversation he expended, perhaps, more true strength than in the pulpit discourse. Possessed of a strong social nature, and gifted with rare conversational powers, his delighted visitors hung for hours on the wisdom and eloquence of his lips. We do not compare him with Johnson or Coleridge, who as conversationalists won so great a fame. Mr. Campbell conversed on different themes and to a widely different circle of hearers. But we doubt if any of his age excelled him in capacity to charm and instruct in the social circle. Perhaps more prejudice was dissipated and more adherents were gained, in these daily conversations, than in his best pulpit efforts.[1]*

Such was the charm of his manner, and the wisdom of his

---

[1] A.S. Hayden, *Early History of the Disciples in the Western Reserve*, page 49.

utterance, that on his tours about the country, wherever he might sojourn for the night, throngs would collect to hear him talk.

> *Nobody wished to talk in his presence. His themes were so much out of the range of ordinary conversation that but few people could sustain a part in their discussion. A question would sometimes set him a-going, but very soon his vast learning, especially in the department of Biblical lore, would lead him into wide fields of discourse, all familiar and easy to him, but strange and unknown to his hearers; and it was their pleasure to sit in silence and learn.*

No matter what the theme of conversation when he entered the circle, or who the company, sooner or later, by the power of his superior genius, all would be hushed into silence while he talked of the love and mercy of God as manifested in the Gospel.

In spite of his great labors, managing an extensive farm with a skill that rivaled his neighbors; writing, editing, and publishing magazines and books that are still a living force in society; teaching and training young men in a manner that made him unrivaled as an educator, and attending with regularity to his pulpit ministrations, where he unfolded the splendors of his great mind, the prince of preachers,—in spite of all these and other burdensome duties, he always found leisure to entertain his guests. His manner was always characterized by such an apparent freedom from preoccupation that one would have little suspected the immense business constantly resting upon him. Visitors were welcomed with unstudied courtesy, and at once put at ease with his hearty greetings and genial pleasantry. But whatever the occasion of their coming, none were permitted to leave his presence without feeling the impress of some great scriptural truth which was at the time resting upon his heart.

One cannot but wonder how the dispenser of such hospitality could carry on the extensive labors that demanded his attention. Nothing but the capacity for intense application and an economical distribution of time, could have made it possible.

From youth he had trained himself in early rising. In this way he was able, in the midst of the constant demands of daily intercourse, to appropriate hours of time that were free from interruption, and when his mind was fresh and would quickly respond to the task set it to perform. I cannot do better than quote the eminent Dr. Richardson's description of his usual manner of employing his time when at home:

> *His habit of rising very early, usually at three o'clock, gave him much valuable time well suited for composition, and at the hour when the house-bell rang for morning worship, he would come over from his study, having prepared, often, enough manuscript to keep his printers busy during the day. When breakfast was over, after arranging the affairs of the morning and kindly seeing off any parting visitors, he would call for a horse, or set off on foot, perhaps accompanied by some of his friends, to view the progress of the printing or the farming operations and give instructions to his workmen. Delighting greatly in agriculture and its collateral pursuits, he was familiar with all their details, and while ever eager to gain new thoughts from others, the most skillful farmers and breeders of stock often found in his company that they had themselves something yet to learn.*
>
> *After dinner he usually spent a little time in correcting proof sheets, which he often read aloud if persons were present; and then he would perhaps have a promised visit to pay to one of the neighboring families in company with his wife or some of the guests. Otherwise he would often spend some hours in his study, if engaged on any important theme, or occupy himself in his portico or parlor in reading or conversation.*[1]

But it was after the labors of the day had ended and the hush

---

[1] *Memoirs of Alexander Campbell*, Vol. 2, page 300.

and quiet of evening had gathered round, that the Bethany home presented its most charming aspect. Let another who often shared its rich spiritual delights describe the scene:

> *At nightfall he collected his family in his homely parlor, and arranged them in order around the room. Each then read a verse, he reading with the rest. In this reading every soul in his house was expected to take part, from the Indian boy of the wild prairies of the West,[1] to the elegant guest of his hospitable home. The chapter for the evening being read, a song was usually sung, when all bowed in the presence of God. His prayers were usually long, inimitably reverential and chaste. At times they were broad and grand. All this was repeated in the morning. In the intervals in the social circle, Christ and the Gospel were the never-ending themes of his conversation. On these he never flagged himself, nor wearied his delighted hearers. These conversations were often relieved by bursts of eloquence, which even his finest flights in the pulpit never surpassed. Yet his manner was as easy and natural as that of a child.[2]*

It will be seen from this picture that the same religious atmosphere in which he had been nurtured from childhood pervaded his home. No matter how busy the day or how urgent the claims upon his time, he always had time for morning and evening devotions with his family and guests.

Nothing was more beautiful than Mr. Campbell's devotion to his family. Whether at home or abroad, wife and children were always the objects of his solicitous care. Following the bereavement which overtook him in 1827 in the death of his companion, he was married to Miss Selina Bakewell, who continued to maintain the reputation of Bethany mansion, and

---

[1] Mr. Campbell, out of sympathy for the Indian race, obtained a boy of the Iowa tribe, and kept him several years in his family, giving him every advantage of secular and religious instruction.

[2] *Lard's Quarterly*, Vol. 3, page 265.

who, after a companionship of nearly forty years, lingered by the fireside, hallowed by his memory, until recently summoned to join him on the other shore, at the extreme age of 95. Often was he called to pass under the rod of affliction in the loss of those whom God had given him. In referring to his bereavements in the *Harbinger* of 1848, Mr. Campbell writes:

How strange, and yet how mournfully pleasing, the thought that of the fourteen children given to me, nine of them are now present with the Lord! Three of them died, never having sinned in their own persons. And as by Adam the first they died, by Adam the second they shall live in the Lord. Six of them died in faith and rejoiced in the hope of a glorious immortality. This, to us, their survivors, is a sovereign balm, a blest relief. Though dead to us, they live with God.

Often as these afflictions came to cast their shadow across his hearthstone, they never for a moment crushed out his inner joy and confidence in God.

His correspondence during the long journeys that often took him from home, breathe a pure and exalted spirit of paternal solicitude and devotion. During his tour in the State of New York, in 1836, he wrote to his wife and daughters:

Dearly Beloved: Next to my own personal and eternal salvation through my Lord and Saviour, there is nothing on earth dearer to me than your present spiritual and eternal good. I wish you to be intelligent, pure, and influential on earth, loving and beloved as far as mortals like you can be; be ornaments to the Kingdom of Jesus Christ, respectful and respected, honorable and honored, good and happy as my wife and daughters ought to be. On you all God has bestowed good mental capacities, powers of acquiring and communicating knowledge, fine feeling and many excellencies capable of much improvement and of rendering you very useful in society. Now let me say to you that you are thereby under great responsibilities, and let me remind you that you all seek to be more intelligent, more amiable, and more exemplary every day. I do not say this as though I did not think you as much so now as any of my wide and extended acquaintances, but because I wish you to be of unrivaled excellence.[1]

A deep tone of religiousness, as in his conversation, pervades his correspondence. His eye was always raised above the common things of earth "as seeing Him who is invisible." Tender, affectionate, congenial in his nature, he never hesitated to yield the peaceful enjoyments of the fireside when his Master needed his service elsewhere. In a letter to his wife, written from Saratoga, he says:

To one who so much loves his wife and his children, and the whole family circle, and delights in making them happy, it is not an easy task to forsake them all for so long a time, but when I think of Him who forsook the Palace of the Universe and the glory of his Father's court, and condescended to be born of a woman and to live in an unfriendly world, and to be treated a thousand times worse than I have ever been, to save us from our sins, I think but little of all I have done or can do to republish his salvation and to call sinners to reformation, and to build up the cause of life, of ancient Christianity.[2]

Later, from the far away South, comes the same longing for home, chastened and subdued by the certain prospect of a heavenly abiding place. From New Orleans, in 1857, he writes:

I am still more attached to home the farther I am from it. There is no place on earth to me like it. But we have no continuing city here, and should always act with that conviction. We should feel that, wherever we are and whatever we do, we are on our journey home.

---

[1] *Memoirs of Alexander Campbell*, Vol. 2, page 412.
[2] *Memoirs of Alexander Campbell*, Vol. 2, page 417.

There is nothing beneath the home of God that can fill the human heart, and that should ever rule and guide and comfort us. I do not think I will ever again undertake so large a journey, or expose myself to so much labor and privation as I am now subjected to. Still, so long as I can do good at home or abroad, it is my duty to do it. I miss your company more than any privation I have to endure. Still, where and when duty calls, it is my wish to obey and deny myself. That same Eye that has watched over us both, and guided and guarded us through life, will, I humbly trust, guard and guide us to the end of life's weary journey.[1]

How beautifully the grand nature of Alexander Campbell is set off by these simple touches of sympathy and affection! His was not the greatness that repels, that dwells serenely on the mountain-top away from his fellows, but the greatness that descends into the valley to help, to encourage our suffering race, and that draws them to himself that he may lead them to Christ.

---

[1] *Memoirs of Alexander Campbell*, Vol. 2, page 628.

Chapter Fifteen:
CLOSING LABORS

Our survey of the life-work of Alexander Campbell has brought us to an age when most men crave rest and release from burdensome duties; but his life was so inseparably linked with the fortunes of the movement he had inaugurated, that he found it impossible to retire to the quiet shades of his Bethany, as he longed to do. Large demand continued to be made upon his time and energies, in the development and encouragement of the great brotherhood as, in a peculiar sense, their leader in the work of religious reformation. So, notwithstanding the weight of increasing years, he continued incessantly to labor for the promotion of the cause that had already consumed the best years of his life.

Through the monthly numbers of the *Millennial Harbinger*, he continued to preach to increasing thousands, unfolding the great plan of human redemption in all its details, with a richness and power that remain unrivaled in the achievements of religious journalism; but which, in his own judgment, came so far short of the sublime reality, that when, at length, he laid down his pen, it was with the confession:

There is a fullness of joy, a fullness of glory, and a fullness of blessedness, of which no living man, however enlightened, however enlarged, however gifted, ever found or entertained one adequate conception.

As the storm of his fierce conflict with sectarianism subsided, he turned his attention to the enlargement of the vision and purposes of those who looked to him for instruction and guidance.

The student who turns from the *Christian Baptist* to the *Millennial Harbinger* will be surprised at Mr. Campbell's apparent change of attitude respecting modern agencies employed in the dissemination of truth. In the former, missionary societies, Sunday-schools, and even Bible societies, come in for his severest criticism and condemnation. In the latter he becomes the friend and champion of each, recognizing them as most efficient and essential factors in the conversion of the world. His early opposition to missionary and other auxiliaries of the church had never, in fact, sprung from objection to method, but because he believed that the methods, when employed by sectarian zeal, increased the hold of religious error on society and contributed to the confusion of mankind. "To convert the heathen," says he, "to the popular Christianity of these times would be an object of no great consequence, as the popular Christians themselves, for the most part, require to be converted to the Christianity of the New Testament." But as he witnessed the growth of a new society pledged to the restoration of the primitive faith, he at once realized that if his followers were to occupy a place of permanence and power in the religious world, it would be by the cultivation of a zealous missionary spirit and a practical acceptance of the great commission in its broadest significance. No sooner, therefore, had the work of establishing the movement been fairly inaugurated, than he began to urge the importance of cooperation in world-wide missions. Under Mr. Campbell's fostering care, in 1849, the American Christian Missionary Society was organized at Cincinnati, and he was at once chosen as its president, a position which he held until the close of his life. With him an interest in the conversion of mankind was inseparably linked with a true apprehension of the Gospel of Christ. He said:

> *The missionary institution is the genuine product of the philanthropy of God our Savior. It is the natural offspring of Almighty love shed abroad in the human heart; and, therefore, in the direct ratio of every Christian's love he is possessed of a missionary spirit.*

These obligations it was his constant delight to enforce. The key-note of his later essays and addresses is contained in the following extract from his annual address before the Christian Missionary Society in 1853:

> *This missionary enterprise is, by universal conces-*

sion, as well as by the oracles of God, the grand work of the ages, the grand duty, privilege, and honor of the church of the nineteenth century. God has by his providence opened up the way for us. He has given us learning, science, wealth, and knowledge of the condition of the living world,—of the pagan nations, their languages, customs, rites, and usages. He has given us the earth, with all its seas, lakes, rivers, and harbors. He has, in the arts and improvements of the age, almost annihilated distance and time, and by our trade and commerce we have, in his providence, arrested the attention and commanded the respect of all heathen lands, of all creeds and of all customs. Our national flag floats in every breeze; our nation and our language command the respect, almost the homage, of all the nations and peoples on earth. God has opened the way for us,—a door which no man or nation can shut. Have we not, then, as a people, a special call, a loud call, a divine call, to harness ourselves for the work, the great work—the greatest work of man—the preaching of the Gospel of eternal life to a world dead, spiritually dead, in trespasses and sins?[1]

The breadth of Mr. Campbell's sympathies in the work of evangelization he thus expresses:

We are encouraged to raise an ensign, to establish a mission, and to invite to our Zion the frozen Icelander and the sunburned Moor, the Indian and the Negro, the Patagonian and the nations of the isles of the ocean.

From the halls of Bethany College he continued, from year to year, to send out an army of young men, trained and equipped to carry forward the work which he had so auspiciously begun. His hope of the ultimate success of the refor-

---

[1] *Popular Addresses,* page 522.

mation was, as we have seen, in an educated ministry. In the accomplishment of this result, the closing years of his life were largely spent in the interests of the institution he had founded, an institution devoted to the study of God's Word as well as letters. We have seen something of the tirelessness with which he pursued his purpose, traveling up and down the country in the heat of summer and the cold of winter,—at times cheered by the hearty and generous response that met his solicitation, again all but cast down by the illiberality of others. At last, after many years of toil and travel, he felt that the goal was almost reached. On a December evening he sat in that congenial circle that gathered around the Bethany fireside, feeling that his labors had largely been completed, and that there remained for him a well-earned repose, released from the wearing toils that had consumed his over-crowded years. But in this he was destined to disappointment. An unforeseen calamity befell his beloved Bethany, that for a moment seemed to dash his hopes and paralyze his energies. On the morning of Dec. 10, 1857, the college buildings were laid in ashes. The achievement of many years of labor was in ruins, the dream of a life-time dashed to the ground.

Many men at Mr. Campbell's age would have given up in despair, or turned the work of rebuilding over to stronger hands. But his great soul soon rose above the discouraging surroundings, and re-gathering his courage he started out again, taking up his tireless journey for funds to rebuild the institution. In setting out upon this mission, Mr. Campbell declared:

> *Nothing but the absolute necessity which seems to be laid upon me by the burning of our college building, libraries, apparatus, etc., could induce me at this season and at my time of life, with the many pressing demands calling for my presence at home, to undertake the arduous labors which are now placed before me. If I did not feel that it is the Lord's work, and that he will be my helper, I would shrink from the task. I sometimes feel like asking to be relieved from further services, but it seems I cannot hope to rest from my*

labors till I am called also to rest with my fathers.
Such as they are, or may be, therefore, all my days
shall be given to the Lord.[1]

With a herculean effort, and after weary months of travel and solicitation, Mr. Campbell was enabled to witness, in the summer of 1858, the laying of the corner-stone of the present beautiful structure, having secured a sufficient sum to assure its completion. In his efforts to increase the resources and influence of the college, he then continued to labor until the gathering of the war cloud in 1861 rendered further effort for the time useless.

In the meantime his pen was always busy. Awake to the dangers of society, interested in whatever offered to contribute to human happiness, his sympathy went out in every movement that would bless his fellowmen and lead them nearer the cross. The Evangelical Alliance, organized for the promotion of union and fellowship among churches, met his hearty approval. He regarded it as another step toward the realization of his dream of a united Christendom, and hailed it as the herald of a better era. The temperance cause, which had begun to absorb a larger share of attention, received his sanction and support. He believed in using all resources in disarming this monster of iniquity, and looked upon prohibition as the only effective remedy for this prolific and manifold evil.

The enforced retirement which age and the throes of our great civil war placed upon him was spent, while strength would permit, in literary pursuits. At the urgent request of an admiring public, he gathered together his addresses upon various literary, social, and religious topics, and published them in a large volume entitled, *Popular Lectures and Addresses*. These had been delivered at college commencements, before literary societies, and in lyceum courses, and represent Mr. Campbell in his best style. They are models of classic English, rich in diction, profound in thought, and religious in tone. His latest literary effort, and one that sadly reflects the decline of

---

[1] *Memoirs of Alexander Campbell*, Vol. 2, page 533.

his intellectual powers, was a volume to the memory of his father, published in 1861. The tribute which he here sought to pay to the character and worth of Thomas Campbell was deserved. It was through his father's fearless loyalty to a high purpose that Mr. Campbell found a field prepared for the exercise of his great gifts. Under Thomas Campbell's tuition, the first lessons in the sublime doctrines of Christian unity were taught, which it was the province of his illustrious son to apply in the organization and development of a great brotherhood, whose chief aim should be the effectual reunion of all Christ's followers under one banner. *The Life of Thomas Campbell* was a grateful recognition of his invaluable contribution to this cause.

One by one those who stood about the reformer in the heat of his religious battles were now being called from their labors. Thomas Campbell, Barton W. Stone, John T. Johnson, William Hayden, and Walter Scott, staunch and tried friends, had preceded him to their reward. He, almost alone, survived of that generation of men who had endured the toil and hardship of the planting; and he, no longer the physical and intellectual giant that had endured the fatigue of an unpopular cause and commanded the admiration of friend and foe alike, awaited the summons of the Master. Body and mind were gradually giving way. Two events seem to have hastened the breakdown of his overtaxed powers. One was the sudden death of his favorite son, Wickliffe, a blow which he accepted with Christian resignation, but from the effects of which he never entirely rallied. The other was the overtaxing labor of translating the Acts of the Apostles for a new version of the Scriptures brought out by the American Bible Union. Before the last, added to his incessant labors along other lines, "he staggered, then he fell, no more to rise to the height of his former power."

One by one he was compelled to relinquish his labors. Early in 1865, after having served as editor of the "Millennial Harbinger" for thirty-five years, he surrendered his position to younger and stronger hands. In the autumn of that year he entered the pulpit for the last time, preaching with unwonted unction and power, electrifying his audience with the beauty of his thought and the earnestness of its presentation. His opening message, delivered more than half a century earlier, declaring and defending the claims of the Word, had been prophetic of his triumphant defense of the sole authority of the Scriptures. His closing message, dwelling in eloquent terms upon "the spiritual blessings in heavenly places in Christ," was likewise prophetic of the change that awaited him. "Do you think," said he, as he was about to step down from the pulpit on this occasion, "do you think, that there is any standstill point in heaven? No; the soul is ever onward, thirsting for the fountains of righteousness that make glad the city of our God." In this hope he calmly and serenely awaited the summons.

The close was befitting the character and life-work of this great man. Death had no terrors to him. It was a birth into the better life beyond. Gradually his strength failed. When no longer able to quit his room or his bed, friends gathered around, cheered by the expressions of heavenly trust that were constantly escaping his lips. Only a week before his death, on Sunday afternoon, while many sat by his bedside, he spoke to them for more than three hours in most eloquent words, at times with all the grandeur and vigor of his prime. A letter dated from his bedchamber by one who watched in the gathering shadows which death was throwing about him, reveals the greatness of his passing spirit:

> *His gentleness and patience mid his suffering break all our hearts. Such sweetness and submission to the slightest wish of others around him.—such kind consideration for everyone who comes into his presence,—his little expressions of greeting, and his inquiry after the welfare of those who come to see him, and such putting away of personal complaint or suffering, move every beholder to tears. All this could never be seen in a character less great and grand than his. He is himself noble and good and great, as nature made him, to the very last. The commanding and fascinating elements of his character are intact in the midst of the wreck of matter. Such passages of*

Scripture as he has recited, even in his wanderings, and such grand sentences as have fallen from his lips—such beautiful soliloquies upon the fleetness of time and upon doing good while we can, etc., are wonderful, very wonderful to us all.[1]

As the end drew near, with Christian assurance his companion said to him: "The blessed Savior will go with you through the valley of the shadow of death." Looking earnestly into her face, he said with great effort, "That he will! That he will." These were his last words. As the hour of midnight approached, on Sunday, March 4, 1866, his spirit took its flight, leaving behind as his heritage to mankind a plea for the reunion of Christ's people upon the principles of his revealed Gospel.

---

[1] *Millennial Harbinger*, 1866, page 207.

Chapter Sixteen:
HIS PLACE IN HISTORY

I come now to the more difficult part of my task, the estimate of the man. There are two standards of measurement upon which that estimate may be formed,—his impress upon his own times, and his influence upon future generations. Measured by either standard, Alexander Campbell was an extraordinary man.

Few men have ever lived to witness larger returns from their labors than he. While he lived in advance of the religious thought of his age, he was, nevertheless, able to interpret the heavenly vision that burst upon his soul with such simplicity, and with such cogency of reason, that the humblest thinker, who was willing to listen to his message, became convinced of its correctness. In this respect his experience differed from that of other men, who, like him, have stood upon the mount of vision, but have been suffered to end their existence in solitary grandeur; uncared for and unappreciated by the men to whom their message was delivered, and to whose sacrifice and service future generations have been left to render tardy justice.

Alexander Campbell, on the other hand, was happy from the very beginning in the fellowship of kindred spirits; and after the first storm of abuse and misrepresentation which assailed him, gradually grew in favor with his own times, and was permitted to enjoy a goodly degree of respect and appreciation even from those who differed with him most widely.

The secret of his popularity is not difficult to discover. To an attractive personality was added the charm of spiritual nobility. He bore the stamp of moral and intellectual integrity, which is the spring of human greatness. Men who met him in social intercourse, or heard him in public address, were impressed with his sincerity and admired his frankness. His attempt to deal fairly and candidly with those who differed with him was one of his marked characteristics, even in the heat of public debate.

Another prominent and distinguishing trait was his reverence for God and sacred things. Before the majesty of the Son of God, he ever bowed in deepest humility and holiest adoration.

> *I noticed while a student at Bethany College,* writes one of his admirers, *that Mr. Campbell, in time of public worship, if he himself was not in the pulpit conducting the services, always knelt during prayer. He never stood. He literally "bowed his knees to the Father of our Lord Jesus Christ." He was pre-eminently a religious man, pious, spiritual, and devout at all times. Many, judging from his debates and writings of controversial character, might suppose that he lacked piety, spirituality, and prayerfulness; but personal acquaintance with him always reproved such supposition. His faith made him happy. He rejoiced in being a Christian.* [1]

But the most conspicuous element of greatness in Mr. Campbell, and the one which rallied admiring multitudes about him, was the greatness of his intellect. In resources of mind he was unrivaled, and he looked the intellectual giant that he was every inch. As he one day walked the streets of London, a stranger, impressed by his commanding presence, was heard to remark: "There goes a man who has brains enough to govern all Europe." The following picture, from the pen of Moses E. Lard, is not overdrawn:

> *His head I think the finest I ever saw. It was simply faultless. After the first look you never criticized it; you only admired it. You dwelt on it only to wonder how magnificently nature sometimes works. His head never disappointed you. No matter with reference to what you studied it, it always complemented your highest expectations. Was it the abode of a mind of extraordinary strength? Every conformation of it answered, "Yes." Was it filled with a soul of profound*

---

[1] *Millennial Harbinger*, 1868, page 205.

religious devotion? The answer was the same. Did it betoken that its occupant was marred by any dangerous or unlovely eccentricities? Not one. Every point, angle, and curve on it revealed that nice adjustment of faculty to faculty which renders greatness safe, and assigns to it its true position in the lead of earth's great beneficent changes. On once looking on that large, finely-turned head, you never feared to trust it more.[1]

Thus endowed by nature and education, Mr. Campbell's unselfish devotion to truth and his able defense of that which he found revealed in the Word of God, speedily made him the popular idol of that class who were longing to see the restoration of Mary's Son to a throne high above councils and creeds. His mission was that of a truth-seeker, rather than the advocate of a doctrine. In this pursuit his religious life was marked by constant change and development. We have seen how even in youth his spirit chafed under the creed-system, in which he had been conscientiously reared; how his restless nature determined upon an independent search after the wisdom of God, first throwing off the yoke to all humanly devised systems; how his pathway, in the light of the revealed will of God, gradually led him to the adoption of new practices and customs, until he found himself without a place in any organized religious society; and how, at last, the creed and practice of the primitive church revealed to him the only course which he could conscientiously and consistently pursue.

In his protest against religious error, he was not simply a reformer, he was more than a reformer. Instead of trying to put a new piece of cloth into the old, worn-out garment of theology, he cast it aside altogether for one which, though ancient, was without rent, and as strong and beautiful as when first wrought out by the hand of God. Instead of reformation he attempted *restoration,*—to replant in the fertile soil of the nineteenth century the church of the first century. The system to which he

---

[1] *Lard's Quarterly*, Vol. 3, page 256.

was thus led to give his influence was in no sense the creation of his genius. The only genius he ever claimed was that of discovery, and even in this he made no original discoveries. "The truth which he discovered had already been revealed, and lay imbedded in the sacred page."

Even after the plea for the restoration of primitive Christianity had fully taken possession of his heart, he continued to advance along many lines of Christian progress. At first he seemed in danger of missing the warmth and spirit of the Gospel message, and of falling into a narrow, legalistic groove that would have checked the progress of truth and defeated the very object he sought to accomplish. His antagonism to Sunday schools, missionary societies, a settled ministry, etc., which marked the early stages of the movement, threatened for a time to limit its growth. But in its later development these came in for his most cordial sympathy and support.

When the zenith of his life had been reached, Mr. Campbell's attitude toward all lines of moral and religious progress was such as to win for him the highest praise of all who were acquainted with his untiring service. I cannot better summarize the impression which he made upon his own times than by quoting from the pen of Leo. D. Prentice, the talented editor, a half century ago, of the *Louisville Journal*:

> *Alexander Campbell is unquestionably one of the most extraordinary men of our time. Putting wholly out of view his tenets, with which we of course have nothing to do, he claims, by virtue of his intrinsic qualities as manifested in his achievements, a place among the very foremost spirits of the age. His energy, self-reliance and self-fidelity, if we may use the expression, are of the stamp that belongs only to the world's first leaders in thought or action. His personal excellence is certainly without a stain or a shadow. His intellect, it is scarcely too much to say, is among the cleanest, richest, profoundest ever vouchsafed to man. Indeed, it seems to us that in the faculty of abstract thinking—in, so to say, the sphere*

of pure thought—he has few if any living rivals. Every
cultivated person of the slightest metaphysical turn,
who has heard Alexander Campbell in the pulpit or in
the social circle, must have been impressed by the
wonderful facility with which his faculties move in the
highest planes of thought. Ultimate facts stand forth
as boldly in his consciousness as sensations do in that
of most other men. He grasps and handles the highest,
subtlest, most comprehensive principles as if they
were the liveliest impressions of the senses. No poet's
soul is more crowded with imagery than his is with the
ripest forms of thought. Surely the life of a man thus
excellent and gifted is a part of the common treasure
of society. In his essential character he belongs to no
sect or party, but to the world.[1]

What will be the ultimate effect of Alexander Campbell's
life-work upon religious society can only be conjectured from
what has already been achieved. Though less than the third of a
century has passed since he ceased from earthly labors, the
permanent benefit of his gift to religious thought is generously
conceded. The little church at Brush Run, over which Mr.
Campbell was the presiding genius, has grown into a great
Christian brotherhood, more than a million strong, with a score
or more of educational institutions, with a current literature
second to none, with mission stations encircling the globe. But
these facts and figures, remarkable as they appear, are among
the least of the results that have followed the labors of this man.
A much larger religious circle, while not consenting to accept
his leadership, are adopting many of the principles for which he
so vigorously contended, and are working out along kindred
lines the great problems that consumed his energies. The
awakening spirit of religious unity, the slackening of party
cords, the growing indifference to the claims of creeds, and the
increasing regard for the message of Christ and his apostles,—these are but the widening circles of a wave set in motion

---

[1] *Memoirs of Alexander Campbell*, Vol. 2, page 639.

by this sturdy champion of the primitive Faith.

It is yet perhaps too soon to assign Mr. Campbell his proper place among the world's religious leaders. A figure so colossal can only be rightly estimated when viewed through the perspective of advancing generations. Shall his name be placed along with those of the other great reformers, Luther, Wickliffe, Calvin, and Wesley, or shall he be placed among stars of lesser magnitude? Time alone will answer. But in view of the achievements that have already been wrought out through his influence, we believe that when the final roll-call has been read, it will be found that to Alexander Campbell has been assigned no secondary place among the heroes who have contributed to the world-wide conquest of the race to the standard of the Cross.

Other Restoration Movement Books from Cobb Publishing

Brother McGarvey: *The Life of J.W. McGarvey* (W.C. Morro)

They Called Him Superman: *The Life of T.W. Brents* (Kyle Frank)

Toils and Struggles of the Olden Times: *Autobiography of Elder Samuel Rogers*

The Life of Elder "Raccoon" John Smith (John Augustus Williams)

A Life Richly Lived: *The Story of Tolbert Fanning* (Kyle Frank)

The Life of Knowles Shaw, Singing Evangelist (William Baxter)

Alexander Campbell: A Collection

Abner Jones: A Collection

These books and more can be purchased from Cobb Publishing (see contact information at the front of the book) or on Amazon.com and CobbPublishing.com

www.ingramcontent.com/pod-product-compliance
Lightning Source LLC
Chambersburg PA
CBHW072014040426
42447CB00009B/1623

9 781947 622050